Stick to Local Farms Cookbook

By Maria Reidelbach

Corn Cow Books

Library of Congress info: Gia doles maximet ea doluptatur? Ga. Equi similit aectotatur, es que simi, sequodi dolupta tibusaperum quaestibeati dolo et id quae laboriaectem accuptatatem rae min expliquia vellore pernatur, quiate repe reribus dantia conse dolla nonseque voluptatis si consed moditas alis voluptatempe velitati alictae cabore comnimos eos simi, omniaerae venihitium est as sundae optat omnimol uptate nim sediant

Design by Maria Reidelbach

10 9 8 7 6 5 4 3 2 1

PRESS CONTACT:

Maria Reidelbach, m@corncow.com, 646-242-6464

Contents

10 Great Reasons to
Eat Locally Grown Food

1. Local food tastes and looks better.
Crops marketed close to home are picked at their peak and are usually sold within a day. Other produce travels on trucks or planes and is stored in warehouses.

2. Local food supports local families.
The wholesale prices that farmers get for their products are usually very low, sometimes not more than the cost of producing them. Local farmers who sell directly to consumers cut out the middleman and can earn a living.

3. Local food builds trust.
With all the issues related to food safety, there's an assurance that comes from looking a farmer in the eye, or seeing the fields where your food comes from.

4. Local food builds community.
When you buy direct from a farmer, supporting a local business and getting to know folks who grow your food. Some farms welcome visitors to share in the changing seasons on the farm.

5. Local food preserves open space.
When farmers get paid more for their products from nearby shoppers, they're less likely to sell farmland for development.

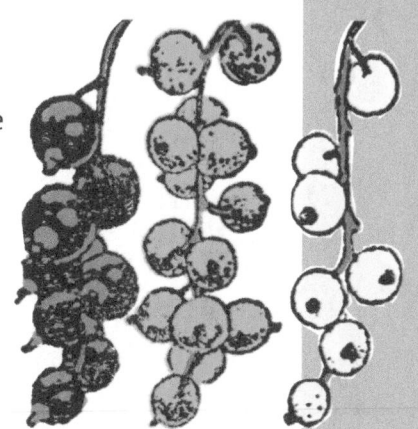

6. Local food keeps taxes down.

According to several studies, farms contribute more in taxes than they require in services.

7. Local food benefits the environment & wildlife.

Small farmers use more environmentally sound growing practices. Local farmers encompass a patchwork of fields, meadows, woods, streams, and ponds that provide essential habitat for wildlife.

8. Local food makes a lighter carbon footprint.

On average our food travels 1,500 miles from farm to plate. Purchasing locally-grown food is a simple way to avoid supporting the increasing expense of fossil fuels and the adverse effects of global warming from increased carbon emissions.

9. Local food adds variety and preserves genetic diversity.

In industrial agriculture, plants are bred for their ability to ripen on cue, withstand harvesting, packing, and storage, and so there are only a few varieties in production. Smal local farms, in contrast, support genetic diversity and often grow many varieties to provide a longer season, an array of colors, and the best flavors.

10. Local food for a better future.

When you buy locally grown food, you're helping to preserve the strength and character of our community for our children and grandchildren.

Adapted from a Mass. Dept. of Agricultural Resources poster foraged by Nicci Cagan. Many thanks!

Hudson Valley *Farm Calendar*

This calendar shows the most common produce grown here, and the season in which it usually grows. Be aware that every year is different—sometimes growth is faster or slower, sometimes crops fail completely.

Spring

asparagus, beets, currants: red, black and white, greens: spinach, young kale, arugula, hen's eggs, herbs, lettuce, peas: English, sugar snap and snow, radishes, rhubarb, strawberries

Summer

beets, blackberries, blueberries, broccoli, carrots, cauliflower, celery, cherries, cucumbers, eggplant, garlic, green beans, herbs, kohlrabi, melons, nectarine, onions, peaches, peppers: sweet and hot, plums, new potatoes, raspberries, stone fruit, summer squash, sweet corn, tomatoes, turnips, zucchini

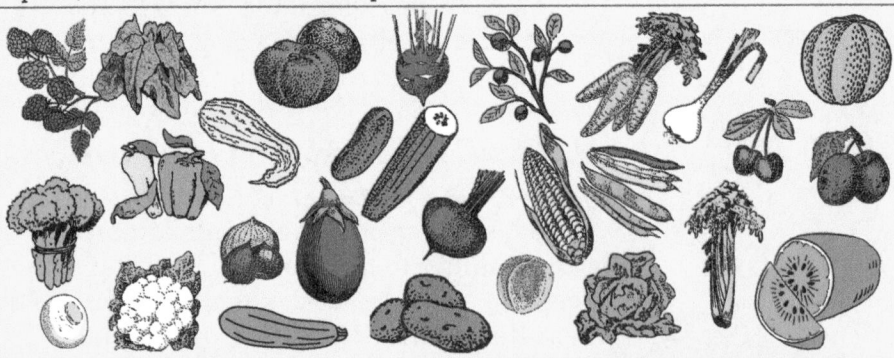

Autumn

apples, beets, broccoli, cabbage, cauliflower, eggs, grapes, greens, herbs, kale, kohlrabi, lettuce, onions, pears, peppers: sweet & hot, potatoes, pumpkins, sweet corn, tomatoes, turnips

Winter

apples, beets, cabbage, carrots, dried beans, eggs, farmed mushrooms, maple syrup, onions, potatoes, winter squash

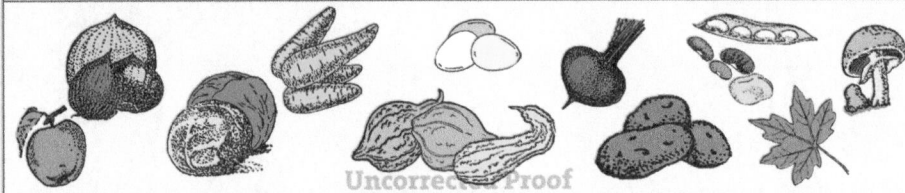

Introduction

Delicious food is one of our primal drives, and eating good food makes me very, very happy. That said, my definition of "good food" has been changing quite a bit. I used to love munching treats like Krispy Kreme doughnuts and Nacho Cheese Doritos (okay, sometimes I still do!). But in recent years I've reevaluated. There are lots of reasons, many of them in the list that opens this book. Another reason is finding out that my favorite processed foods were engineered by food scientists to over-stimulate instinctive food cravings with extremely delicious refined foods. Once turned on, these cravings don't easily shut off. Yipes! Pair this knowledge with the nutritional science that buying whole, unprocessed produce and ingredients and cooking at home is much more healthy, and the best choice seems clear.

Wonderfully, I have found that eating good, locally grown food, in season, is way more luscious than anything whipped up by guys in white lab coats.

The freshest and ripest fruit and vegetables are also the most tasty because that's when they're at their peak of sugars, aromatic oils, and juice. Local fruit and veggies are varieties that are grown for taste, fragrance and texture rather than extremely long shelf life or durability in shipping.

A great example is a brandywine tomato just plucked from the vine—it's warm from the sun, and the piquant scent of the tomato leaves, quite different from the fragrance of tomato, barely clings to the tomato's minutely fuzzy skin. As you take a bite, your teeth burst the thinly stretched skin and your mouth is flooded with sweet, tart, umami juice—an amazing naturally balanced taste treat and yes, it's almost as good as....well, you get my drift. Supermarket tomatoes? They're tough-skinned, dry, and almost tasteless. Yuck!

I've discovered that when I stick to locally grown food I experience and enjoy the seasons of year way more. If I haven't had fresh asparagus for ages, I look forward to the first asparagus of the season—it is exciting and precious. And later, if there's plenty, there's even time for a hedonistic gorge or two (everything in moderation, even moderation). Now, every season and every crop ripening is a little holiday to celebrate!

I love the process of bringing local food to the kitchen, whether it comes from my own little garden plot, it's foraged wild food, or, especially, if it's purchased right from the farmer, at a farmstand, farmers market or pick-your-own. Talking with the folks who grow your food is a great reality check. Farmers may be reserved, but once you make friends they are an amazing font of knowledge and practicality. Plus, farmstands and farmers markets are a great place to hang out, do a little taste-testing, run into neighbors, meet new people, share recipes, even hear music and get other locally made products. And being around all those amazing shapes, colors, scents and textures is exciting in a very elemental way—we are hard-wired by genetics to be happy around good, healthy nourishment.

You can find locally grown food at farmers markets (you can get a list at search.ams.usda.gov/farmersmarkets) at farms (localharvest.org), roadside stands, at some supermarkets and health food stores, and sometimes even flea markets. You can support local farms and share in bumper crops by joining a Community Supported Agriculture, or CSA, farm. In late winter or early spring you pay for a share of the farmer's crop for the rest of the season. Each week you pick up a box of freshly picked produce. Of course, you can even grow your own food—it's easy if you start small. One great way to begin is to grow herbs—they will grow almost anywhere, including in a container, they add lots of nutrition and flavor, and it's nice to always have a variety on hand.

This Book

This is a book of favorite recipes that feature fruit, veggies and herbs that thrive in the Hudson Valley (and lots of other temperate areas of the world). Most are for vegetables and fruit—for optimum health this should be the basis of our diet. Many recipes were collected from the great recipe commons or favorite cookbooks years ago and have been adapted, honed and tweaked. I've chosen recipes that are delicious, simple and forgiving. Most are basics, if there are any fussy parts, they're there for a reason.

I've divided the book into seasons, but lots of vegetables and fruit span seasons, so surf around and check out the index. Plus, there are master recipes that can be made with a wide variety of fruit or veggies.

In my years as a home cook, I've learned some simple ways of making food extra delicious and easy to prepare. Most are pretty basic:

- Be sure to add enough salt—start with ½ teaspoon for every four servings (or 1/8 teaspoon per serving) and keep adding and tasting until you're happy. Kosher salt is a good-tasting all purpose type—iodized salt sometimes tastes like chemicals.

- *❧* Freshly ground black pepper is *the bomb*—and once you buy a grinder, it's no more expensive than stale pre-ground pepper.

- *❧* Always clean fresh greens thoroughly—grit is a real buzz-kill. Fill a salad spinner with water, add only as many greens as can float freely with a little room between and swish them gently around by hand. Slowly lift the basket, allowing the grains of soil to fall to the bottom, empty the water, rinse the bowl, then repeat twice more. Three dunks is the charm!

- *❧* If you don't have a separate sink for washing produce and, like me, you've always got a few dirty dishes lurking in there, a screen basket with a frame that suspends it over your sink is great. You can rinse and spray your veggies above the mess.

- *❧* We are so lucky that olive oil tastes great and is healthy. Don't bother to use pricey extra-virgin olive oil for cooking—once it's heated you can't taste the difference. Save the EVOO for salads or a finishing drizzle.

- *❧* Keep your knives sharp and have plenty of cutting boards around. Get a sharpening stone (they aren't hard to use if you have a steady hand) or a knife sharpener.

- *❧* A garlic press will save the time it takes to mince garlic—the self cleaning ones are best.

- *❧* A couple of wire whisks and heat-resistant silicone spatulas of different sizes are very handy.

- *❧* A stick/immersion blender is an awesome thing! You can makes soups, sauces, and smoothies right in a pot, bowl, pitcher or tumbler. Plus, a stick blender can puree larger volumes than will fit in a blender pitcher.

Most important, relax and have fun. Substitute fruit, veggies and herbs at will in any of these recipes and you'll most likely do just fine—and maybe better. Taste often! Take notes in the margins! (Baking cakes and loaves is a kind of alchemy so it's best to stick to directions.)

The design of these pages is inspired by vintage cooking pamphlets—gorgeous specimens of graphic design from the turn of the 19th century through the 1960s. Just recently I've realized that through these sophisticated publications we were taught to eat processed and imported food! The booklets promoted various brand-name ingredients, like Crisco, exotic produce such as bananas, and new kinds of appliances

like ovens with automatic thermostats. They were so much more colorful and snazzy than the stained and hand-written recipe cards folks made themselves, and they were very seductive. I'm enjoying the irony of swiping their strategy for this effort. The illustrations are almost all foraged and refurbished from my father's WWII-era French-German-Italian picture dictionary and phrase book. This handbook is a catalog of life in a bygone day, and included many fruit and vegetables that disappeared from our plates but are now making a comeback, like kohlrabi and currants.

I hope you enjoy harvesting, making and eating all of our delicious local food as much as I do.

Acknowledgements

[THIS SECTION WILL BE PUT IN NARRATIVE FORM]

Elizabeth Panzer
Lisa Kellogg
Mark Bittman
Faith Willinger
Jean George Vongerichten
Elizabeth Schneider
Rozanne Gold
Alice Waters
Anna Thomas
Darina Allen

Valeriya Sadchikova
Emilia Stern
Barry Koffler
Deborah Artman
Deborah DeWan
Oscar Schnider
Nicci Cagan
Risa Mickenberg
Arthur Zaczkiewicz
RVGA Board

A donation of 3% of the profits of this book will support the Rondout Valley Growers, our farmers and neighbors who advocate, celebrate and keep local farming strong.

Spring

Remarkably, even in the earliest days of Hudson Valley spring, when the snow has just melted and everything looks so beaten up, there is fresh local food to enjoy, and the farmer is Mother Nature. If you've got a wild, weedy place nearby, you can probably find rosettes of garlic mustard and tangles of chickweed. They're both delicious wild greens that you can use in both salad and cooked greens recipes. (Find more info about foraging on-line or in a book.)

Many farms now overwinter spinach so it's up and at'em first thing, too. Other early vegetables are lettuce, sorrel (a lemony-tart green), and even rhubarb, which, with its juicy pink stems, acts like a fruit. Parsley and other early green herbs are a welcome change from dried. Recent research has found that fresh herbs can have 40 times the nutrients of leaf lettuce, so indulge with abandon!

Asparagus is the priapic star of spring—the very earliest shoots are said to be the sweetest, full of sugars stored over the winter in the roots. Shell peas, snow peas, and sugar snap peas are next to arrive, and the greens of pea plants are an amazing treat, too. Spring baby root vegetables, like carrots and beets, are sweet and tender and often have edible greens as well (even carrot greens can be used as an herb).

Strawberries are, of course, awesome, with many dessert possibilities, and pairing well with weirdo rhubarb. Rhubarb has actually got a great flavor on its own and is full of vitamins—a fantastic spring tonic. I've included several great recipes for this under-appreciated plant that thrives in our climate.

Currants bridge the end of spring to summer and they deserve to be more popular. They're easy to grow, come in red, white, pink and black, and they taste almost tropical. The black variety has a complex, winey flavor that I especially love.

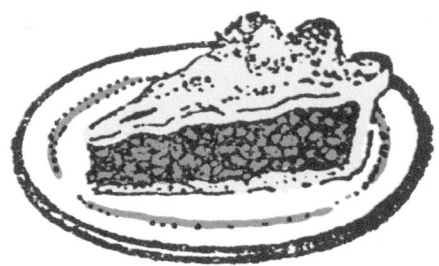

Creamy Asparagus Soup

This soup is so rich, you would think it is made with cream.

2 tablespoons butter
1 cup thinly sliced leeks or onions, white and pale green parts only
½ small russet or other starchy potato, peeled, cut into ½-inch cubes
2½ cups chicken or vegetable stock
3 cups asparagus (about one bundle)
Salt and pepper to taste

Snap the tough ends from the asparagus and, if the ends are fat, peel and keep them. Cut all into 1-inch pieces.

Melt butter in heavy large saucepan over medium heat. Add leek or onion and potato and sauté 2 minutes. Add broth and bring to boil. Reduce heat to medium; cover and cook until vegetables are tender, about 10 minutes. Add asparagus. Simmer uncovered until just tender, 3 to 6 minutes. Remove pan from heat.

Using a countertop or stick blender, purée soup until smooth. Season to taste with salt and pepper. Serve warm or chilled.

4 servings

Bright Greens Soup

A master recipe for a wide variety of spring greens, such as Swiss chard, dandelion greens, watercress, beet greens, spinach and lambs quarters.

2 tablespoons olive oil
2 leeks or onions, sliced
4 garlic cloves, sliced
6 cups chopped greens (leaves only)
Salt and pepper to taste
4 slices bread
1 garlic clove cut in half
Grated Parmesan cheese (optional)

Heat one tablespoon of the oil in a large, heavy soup pot over medium heat, and add the leeks. Cook, stirring, until tender, 3 to 5 minutes. Add the sliced garlic and ½ teaspoon salt, and cook, stirring, until the garlic is fragrant, about 1 minute. Add the greens; stir until they begin to wilt. Add 1 ½ quarts of water and salt to taste; bring to a simmer. Reduce the heat and simmer, partially covered, for 15 to 20 minutes, until the greens are very tender and the broth sweet. Add pepper, taste and adjust seasoning.

Toast the bread. Trim crust off if desired. Rub with the cut side of the halved garlic clove and drizzle with a little more oil, then cut into crouton cubes. Place some croutons in each bowl. Ladle in the soup, sprinkle with some cheese if desired and serve.

8 servings

2½ tablespoons balsamic vinegar
1 teaspoon mayonnaise
Salt and pepper to taste
3 tablespoons olive oil
8 cups of spinach
1½ pound strawberries, cut lengthwise

Whisk together vinegar, mayo, salt and pepper in a small bowl, then add oil in a slow stream, whisking well. Put spinach and strawberries in a large bowl and toss with just enough vinaigrette to lightly coat. Serve immediately.

6 to 8 servings

Spinach Strawberry Salad

Try this with raspberries, too.

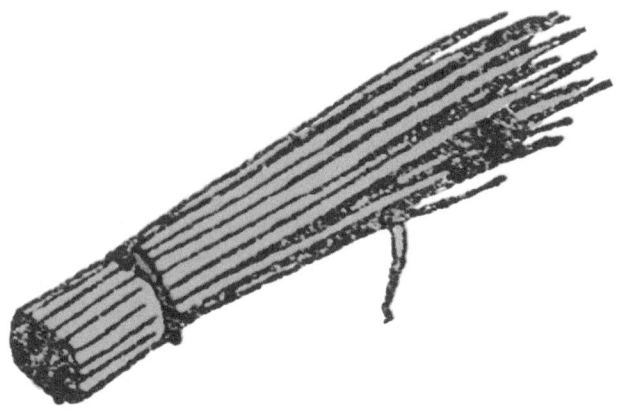

2 pounds asparagus, tough ends snapped
Salt and pepper to taste
¼ cup fresh lemon juice
1 tablespoon Dijon mustard
1 tablespoon honey
1 garlic clove, minced
¾ cup extra-virgin olive oil
1 tablespoon fresh chives, finely chopped

Steam asparagus, shaking once or twice, just until tender, from 3 to 8 minutes depending on thickness. Refresh in cold water. When completely cool, drain and pat dry with paper towels.

Combine lemon juice, mustard, honey, garlic, salt and pepper in bowl. Slowly whisk in oil to emulsify. Stir in chives. Arrange asparagus on platter and drizzle with vinaigrette.

6 servings

Lemon Asparagus Salad

This vinaigrette dressing is also great on green salad or cold salmon.

Roasted Beet and Sugar Snap Pea Salad

Winter and spring produce together—just like spring weather.

3 medium beets, trimmed
1 pound sugar snap peas, trimmed
1 tablespoon Dijon mustard
1 lemon, juiced
¼ cup olive oil
3 tablespoons fresh dill, chopped
1 teaspoon maple syrup or sugar
Fresh salad greens

Cook beets, testing for tenderness by poking with a toothpick:

- Preheat oven to 375°F. Wrap the beets individually or together in aluminum foil. Bake until tender, from 1 to 1 ½ hours.
  OR
- In a saucepan, cover beets with water, bring to a boil and cook until tender, from 30 to 45 minutes.

Cool. Rub the skins off the beets and cut into wedges.

Steam peas until just tender, about 4 minutes. Drain. Rinse with cold water; drain well. Spin or pat dry.

Mix mustard and lemon juice in a small bowl. Gradually mix in oil, then dill and sugar. Toss beets and peas together with the dressing. Serve on a bed of fresh greens.

4 servings

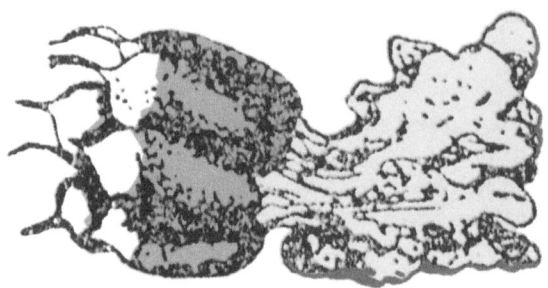

Dijon Dill Salad Dressing

Great on cold, sliced potatoes.

4 teaspoons Dijon mustard
4 teaspoons cider or wine vinegar
¼ cup olive oil
3 tablespoons fresh dill, chopped
1 ½ teaspoons maple syrup or sugar

Whisk mustard and vinegar in small bowl. Gradually mix in oil, then dill and sugar.

About ¾ cup

4

3 tablespoons olive oil
1 large onion, chopped
4 to 5 shallots, chopped
¾ pound spinach, chopped
3 ounces cream cheese, softened at room temperature
2 cups sour cream
Salt and pepper to taste

Heat oil in a 12-inch heavy skillet over moderate heat until hot but not smoking, then sauté onion and shallots, stirring, until lightly browned, about 2 minutes. Continue to cook, stirring occasionally, until softened, about 8 minutes more. Add spinach and cook, stirring, just until wilted, about 2 minutes. Remove from heat and cool slightly.

Transfer spinach mixture to a bowl, then stir in cream cheese, sour cream, salt and pepper to taste until combined well. Cover and chill at least 1 hour.

About 2½ cups

4 scallions or a fistful of chives
¼ cup vegetable oil
2 tablespoons rice vinegar
1 teaspoon soy sauce
1 teaspoon Asian sesame oil
1 garlic clove
½ teaspoon fresh ginger
¼ teaspoon dried, crushed red pepper
Salt and pepper

Roughly chop the white and pale green parts of the scallions. Peel and roughly chop the ginger. Combine all ingredients and purée using blender until smooth. Season to taste with salt and pepper.

About ½ cup

Spicy Korean-Style Dressing

Wonderful for heartier green salads with baby kale, spinach, arugula, mustard greens, etc..

Parsley Walnut Pesto

The first pesto I ever made—back in the 1970s. Serve on pasta, toast, hot or not white beans or chick peas, or steamed vegetables.

3 cups of flat leaf or curly parsley, packed
1 cup of walnuts
3 cloves of garlic
1 cup of extra-virgin or regular olive oil
Salt

Coarsely chop the parsley, walnuts and garlic. Put in a blender or food processor with the oil. Blend until smooth. Add salt to taste.

For a thinner consistency, add water, a teaspoon at a time.

> ✍ Experiment with your own combinations of herbs and nuts. For instance, try half fresh oregano and half parsley with hazelnuts, or marjoram and parsley with almonds. When using stronger-flavored herbs, reduce amount.

Enough for 1 pound pasta, 6 servings

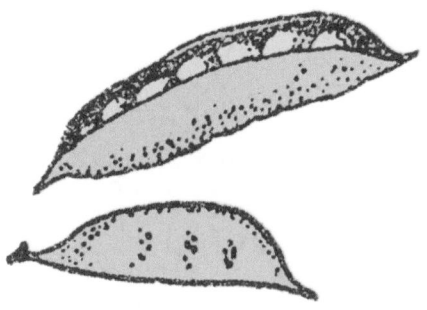

Pea Pesto

An odd idea, but really good. The sweetness of fresh peas makes it. Beautiul on farfalle butterfly pasta.

2 cups fresh shelled peas
2 large garlic cloves
½ cup pine nuts
½ cup grated Parmesan cheese
⅓ cup olive oil
2 tablespoons fresh mint, thyme or parsley, chopped
Salt and pepper to taste

Place peas in a pot with ½ inch of boiling water. Cover and simmer until just cooked, about 2 to 4 minutes. Drain and refresh in cold water.

With food processor running, drop in garlic and finely chop. Turn off motor and add peas, nuts, cheese, mint, ½ teaspoon salt and ½ teaspoon pepper, then process until finely chopped. With motor running, add oil, blending until incorporated.

Serve on pasta.

4 servings

6

1 pound sugar snap peas, stringed
1 teaspoon toasted sesame seeds
1 teaspoon toasted or Asian sesame oil

Steam sugar snap peas until crisp-tender, about 3 minutes. Transfer to a bowl. Toss with seeds and oil. Season with salt.

4 servings

1 cup sour cream
2 tablespoons fresh chives, chopped
2 tablespoons fresh dill, chopped
2 tablespoons cilantro, chopped
1 tablespoon fresh lemon juice

Mix ingredients in small bowl. Season to taste with salt and pepper. Let dip stand 30 minutes at room temperature, or cover and chill until ready to serve, up to one day. Serve dip with raw vegetables like radishes, carrots and pea pods.

About 1 cup

⅓ cup mayonnaise
¼ cup fresh basil, parsley, tarragon or other tender herb leaves
½ cup sour cream
squeeze of fresh lime juice
2 tablespoons fresh chives, finely chopped

In a food processor pulse together all ingredients except the chives until smooth. Garnish dip with chives.

About 1 cup

Sugar Snap Peas and Sesame Seeds

Fast and yummy!

Lemon-Herb Vegetable Dip

This dip just gets better with time—so make it in advance if you wish.

Herb-Chive Dip and Sauce

A delicious for vegetables and great on chicken and fish, too.

Asparagus Lemon Pasta

So good! This is a neat Italian method adapted from Faith Willinger that uses starchy pasta cooking water from the pasta to thicken the sauce.

1 pound asparagus
5 to 6 quarts water
2 to 3 tablespoons salt
1 teaspoon lemon zest, minced or grated
¼ cup olive oil
Salt and pepper to taste
14 to 16 ounces farfalle (butterfly) or other short pasta
½ cup grated Parmesan cheese

Snap the tough ends from the asparagus and, if thick, peel and use them. Cut the asparagus into 1-inch pieces and set aside the tips.

If you've got a pot fitted with a colander, this is the time to use it. Bring 5 quarts of water to a rolling boil, add 2 tablespoons salt and cook asparagus stems for 6 to 8 minutes until soft and tender. Remove stems (keep the water boiling), refresh stems in cold water and drain.

Cook the tips in the boiling water for 3 to 5 minutes until tender, remove (keep water boiling) refresh tips in cold water, and drain.

Add the pasta, and cook ¾ of the recommended cooking time.

While the pasta is cooking, with a food processor or blender, purée the stems with lemon zest, oil, ½ cup asparagus cooking water and salt and pepper to taste.

When the pasta is ready to drain, dip out another cup or so of the cooking water and set aside. Drain the pasta and return it to the empty pot (without the strainer basket). Add the purée, asparagus tips, another ½ cup cooking water and cook over high heat, stirring, until the pasta is almost cooked and sauce coats pasta. Add more pasta water, ¼ cup at a time, if the sauce becomes too dry (it should be a little wet when you're done). Add the grated cheese. Heat just to melt the cheese, and serve immediately.

8 servings as a side dish, 4 as a main dish

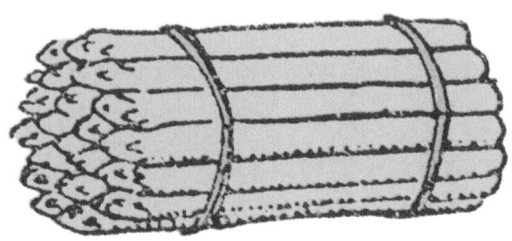

4 tablespoons vegetable oil, add more as needed
4 scallions, chopped
2 pounds vegetables, peeled, trimmed and grated
1 tablespoon ginger or garlic, minced
1 tablespoon curry powder
Salt and pepper to taste

Grate the vegetables coarsely, using a food processor or by hand. Heat 2 tablespoons of oil over medium-high heat. When oil just begins to smoke, add scallions, vegetables, ginger or garlic and curry powder. Cook, stirring, until vegetables begin to brown, about 10 minutes. Add salt and pepper to taste. Serve.

Note: The key to this recipe is choosing the vegetables. Think color and texture. Summer squash and cabbage are tender. Winter squash, potatoes, beets and turnips are hearty. And I like to add asparagus, peas and/or green beans to the grated vegetables when they are in season.

4 servings

1 bunch of asparagus
Vegetable or olive oil
Salt

Break the ends off the asparagus spears: they will naturally snap where the skin becomes tough. Rub them with enough oil to coat the surfaces and sprinkle with salt to taste.

Grill on a medium-hot grill, turning, until lightly browned.

Eat with your fingers. Leftovers are good on sandwiches or sliced into salads.

4 servings

Vegetable Confetti Party

Fun and yummy! And you can use any fresh vegetables from market or garden.

Grilled Asparagus

Grilling asparagus caramelizes the skin. The fatter the stalks, the juicier.

Gingersnap Fruit Tart

Not much cooking needed for this cool spring and summer treat. It's fun to arrange the fruit in elaborate patterns.

1¾ cup ginger snap cookies
¼ cup nuts (optional)
⅓ cup soft butter
1 cup cream cheese at room temperature
¼ cup sugar
1 envelope plain gelatin
1¾ cup juice (white grape or your choice)
1 teaspoon vanilla
4 cups of berries and fruit, sliced or cut into berry-sized pieces

With food processor or blender, crumb the cookies, toss in nuts, then butter. Press evenly into 9-inch pie pan or 10-inch tart pan. If desired, bake at 375°F for 5 minutes.

Cream the cream cheese, sugar and vanilla with an electric mixer or food processor and pour it into the crust.

Empty the gelatin into a bowl and pour ¼ cup of cool juice over. Heat 1 cup of juice to just under boiling and mix with gelatin until dissolved. Mix in remaining juice. Pour ½ over cheese mixture. Arrange the fruit in an even layer, then pour over the remaining gelatin. Chill 4 to 6 hours.

8 servings

Panzers' Easy Fruit Torte

A delicious, versatile recipe for berries, rhubarb, or any type of fruit that is in season. Don't try to shortcut— baking is alchemy!

1 tablespoon sugar
Juice from ½ lemon
1 tablespoon flour (if fruit is juicy)
1 to 2 teaspoons of cinnamon
1 cup sugar
½ cup butter
1 cup flour
1 teaspoon baking soda
Pinch salt
2 eggs
2 cups of fruit, peeled if needed, and cut into bite-sized pieces

Preheat oven to 350°F. Oil and flour a either 9-inch springform pan or a regular cake pan with wax paper cut to fit the bottom.

Mix the first 4 ingredients and set aside.

Cream butter and sugar with an electric mixer on high speed several minutes until light. Add flour, baking soda, salt and eggs. Pour into pan. Spoon the fruit on top and sprinkle with sugar-cinnamon mixture to cover entire surface. Bake for 1 hour.

8 servings

½ cup sugar or maple syrup, more or less, to taste
3 tablespoons butter
2 cups of any fruit or berry: rhubarb, strawberries, blueberries, currants,
    raspberries, blueberries, or other fruit, peeled, hulled, picked over,
    washed, and dried, if necessary
½ teaspoon cinnamon, if desired
Sour cream, créme fraîche, yogurt or whipped cream

In a saucepan heat butter and maple syrup or sugar, plus if using sugar, ½ cup water. Stir until the mixture is thick and syrupy, but not browned.

Add the fruit and optional cinnamon and cook over low heat until the fruit begins to break down and release its juices, about 2 minutes (some fruits will require a little more water).

Serve topped with a dollop of creamy dairy.

2 to 4 servings

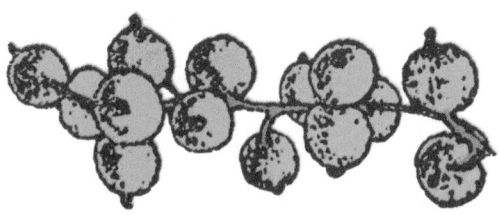

1 cup of maple syrup or ½ cup sugar dissolved in 1 cup hot water
3 cups strawberries, raspberries, blackberries, and/or blueberries
1 tablespoon fresh lemon juice

Purée berries with lemon juice with a blender until smooth, then force through a fine sieve into a bowl to remove seeds. Stir in maple or sugar syrup.

Cover and chill until cold, at least 1 hour.

Freeze in ice-cream maker, then transfer to an airtight container and put in freezer to harden. This mixture makes great whole-fruit popsicles, too.

Experiment with other seasonal fruits and by adding other complementary flavorings like a few tablespoons of Sambuca or other liquor.

1 quart

Warm Fresh Fruit Compote

Great for any ripe local fruit!

Fresh Berry Sorbet

This is a good master recipe for all kinds of berries and fruits.

No-Bake Berry Pie

This pie is fast and fresh on a hot summer day! Try other fruits, too!

1 cup sugar or ¾ cup maple syrup or honey
¼ cup corn starch
7 cups of berries: blueberries, blackberries, raspberries or strawberries
3 tablespoons lemon juice
1 8-inch or 9-inch pie shell, either pre-baked or graham craker

Fill the crust will 6 cups of berries.

Mix sugar, corn starch and lemon juice with remaining berries.

Cook over medium heat for 8 minues until thick and glossy.

Pour over berries and refrigerate for 2 hours.

6 to 8 servings

Cherry Fruit Salad

Cherries, peaches, plums and other stone fruits are all related to almonds, and all have a fragrant bitter almond in the center of their pit.

1 pound cherries, pits removed and set aside
½ cup sugar or maple syrup to taste
¼ pound black or red currants
1 cup Port wine

Crack the cherry pits by smacking them lightly with a hammer or the bottom of a saucepan; you don't need to pulverize them, just expose their centers. Place them in a pot with ½ cup water and the sugar or syrup. Bring to a boil, cook for 2 minutes, cover, then cool while proceeding with the recipe.

Combine the currants and Port in a medium saucepan and bring to a boil over high heat. Reduce by half, stirring occasionally; this will take at least 10 minutes.

Strain the cherry syrup into a saucepan, pressing to extract as much liquid as possible. Then strain into it the currant-Port mixture, without pressing.

Bring to a boil, add the cherries and turn off the heat. Cover and cool, then serve.

6 servings

2 pounds rhubarb, trimmed and cut into 2-inch lengths
1 cup sugar or ¾ cup maple syrup
2 vanilla beans or 1 tablespoon vanilla extract
Optional: strawberry slices, sorbert, yogurt, sour cream

Add the sugar to a quart of water in a saucepan and cook over medium-high heat. Split the vanilla beans lengthwise and scrape out the seeds; add seeds and vanilla pods to the pot. When the mixture boils, reduce the heat to medium, cook for 5 minutes, then add the rhubarb. Cook for another 5 to 10 minutes, until the rhubarb begins to fall apart.

Cool to room temperature, then cover and refrigerate for several hours or overnight.

When you're ready to serve the soup, fish out the vanilla pods and break up the chunks of rhubarb with a spoon or whisk. Serve cold, with slices of strawberry, a scoop of any sorbet, a dollop of yogurt or sour cream, or plain.

4 servings

Rhubarb Soup

A delicious dessert recipe adapted from Jean-Georges Vongerichen and Mark Bittman. It's fun to serve with shortbread cookie "crackers."

---

4 cups of chopped rhubarb
¾ cup maple syrup or ¾ cup sugar and ¼ cup brown sugar
½ cup water

Heat sugars and water or syrup to boiling in 2 quart saucepan, stirring occasionally. Add rhubarb and reduce heat. Simmer uncovered until rhubarb is tender, about 5 to 10 minutes. Refrigerate.

Variation: Simmer to reduce rhubarb to 3 cups. After rhubarb is cooked, add 1 cup halved strawberries. Heat just to boiling.

1 quart, 6 servings

Rhubarb Sauce

Delicious over Cornmeal Pound Cake (page 67) or used as a base for a spread or smoothie (see below)

---

8 ounces cream cheese, room temperature
¼ cup rhubarb sauce (see above)

Combine cream cheese and rhubarb sauce with electric mixer until smooth. Spread on toast, bagels or English muffins.

1 cup

Rhubarb Spread

Rhubarb Smoothie

2 cups rhubarb sauce or the ingredients of rhubarb sauce (see page 13)
2 cups yogurt

Spin with food processor or blender until smooth.

1 quart

Rhubarb Bread

⅓ cup room temperature butter
1 ¼ cups firmly packed brown sugar
2 eggs, slightly beaten
⅓ cup milk
1 teaspoon vanilla extract
2 cup flour
2 teaspoons baking powder
½ teaspoon baking soda
¼ teaspoon salt
1½ cups rhubarb, chopped

Grease two 8-inch loaf pans and preheat the oven to 325°F.

Cream butter and brown sugar using an electric mixer. Gradually add the eggs, beating until fluffy. Add milk and vanilla and blend well. Combine dry ingredients in a separate bowl and add in 3 or 4 parts. Remove from mixer and fold in the chopped rhubarb with a spatula. Pour into 2 greased loaf pans and bake for 45 to 50 minutes or until a toothpick inserted in the center comes out clean. For best flavor, wrap the bread when cool and let stand at room temperature for 24 hours.

2 loaves

3 cups rhubarb, diced
1 cup sugar
3 tablespoons flour
2 eggs
1 8-inch or 9-inch pie shell

Preheat oven to 400°F.

Arrange the rhubarb in unbaked pie shell.

Blend together the sugar and flour, add the eggs and stir.

Pour over the rhubarb. Bake for 20 minutes, then reduce temperature to 350°F and bake 20 minutes. Test center for doneness (it will be firm and custardy).

The filling is also good with a teaspoon of vanilla added and cooked in a baking dish as a custard.

8 servings

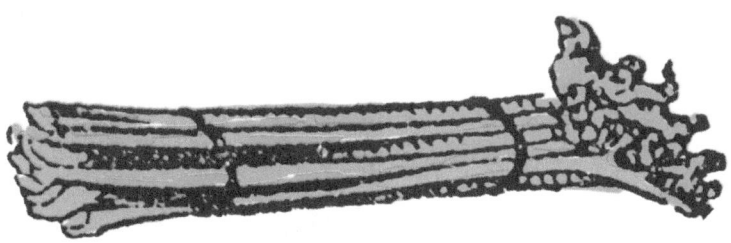

3½ cups rhubarb, cut in ½-inch slices
3½ cups strawberries, hulled and halved
½ cup (packed) brown sugar
½ cup sugar
¼ cup cornstarch or instant tapioca
1 teaspoon ground cinnamon
¼ teaspoon salt
1 9-inch double pie crust

Preheat oven to 400°F. Combine first 7 ingredients in large bowl. Toss gently to blend.

Spoon filling into bottom crust. Lay top crust over the fruit and crimp the edges. Cut several vents. Bake 20 minutes. Reduce oven temperature to 350°F. Continue baking pie until golden and filling bubbles in the center, about 1 hour and 10 minutes more. Transfer pie to rack and cool completely.

8 servings

Aunt Mabel Hillier's Delicious Rhubarb Custard Pie

The tartness of rhubarb is great with rich egg custard.

Strawberry Rhubarb Pie

One of the world's best pies, period. How does it happen that two such companionable flavors both grow in the spring?

Summer

What's not to like about Hudson Valley in the summer? Heavenly, breezy, long days of sun encourage the fields and gardens to really put the "produce" into produce. The fruit harvest begins with cherries, then blueberries, raspberries, blackberries, and more stone fruit: peaches, apricots, a crazy variety of plums plus a rainbow of beautiful melons. Lots of fruits, especially berries, freeze very easily—now's the time to stock up for winter!

We all love fruit—and there's a reason for that. Besides mother's milk, fruit is the only other food that exists especially for us animals to munch, eating both fruit and seed. We then travel on our way, and, sooner or later, we deposit that fruit seed in a nice pat of fertilizer—a great start for a seedling. Many of our most basic instincts are part of our love of fruit, from our attraction to bright, ripe colors to our love of sweetness.

Vegetables, by contrast, are officially the non-seed-bearing plant parts: shoots, leaves, stems, flowers, roots, bulbs and tubers. There are also lots of fruits we consider veggies: tomatoes are one of the most beloved, cucumbers and squash (so closely related to melons), eggplant and peppers. And a summer favorite, sweet corn, is a grain, and technically also a fruit!

One vegetable family I adore is the brassicas, know by farmers as cole crops. At a cabbage family reunion there's an astounding variety of plants and of the parts we eat. We eat the flower buds of broccoli and cauliflower, the leaves of arugula, kale, collards, bok choy, mizuna, and mustard, the stems of broccoli rabe and kohlrabi and the roots of radishes, turnips and rutabaga. We even use the seeds of mustard to make a classic condiment. Many of brassicas come in amazing colors: acid green, deep teal, ivory, yellow, purple and burgundy, all signaling major amounts of different phytonutrients.

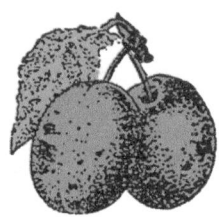

3 medium-sized eggplants
1 to 4 fresh chiles or any fresh hot pepper
¼ cup white onion, finely chopped
¼ cup cilantro, chopped
1 tablespoon fresh lime juice
Salt

Prick eggplants in several places with a fork. Char them and chiles by grilling either over medium-hot coals, on top of a gas cooktop, or under a broiler. Turn them frequently, until chile skins are blistered and charred and eggplants are charred all over and very soft, 5 to 12 minutes for peppers; 18 to 20 minutes for eggplants.

As chiles are cooked, transfer them to a large bowl, cover and let stand 20 minutes. Cool eggplants 15 minutes.

While eggplants cool, carefully rub off skins from chiles. Don't sweat it if you can't get all the black off—it adds flavor. Stem, seed and devein chiles, then chop. Transfer to a large bowl.

Peel eggplants and drain in a colander 10 minutes. Coarsely chop and add to chiles along with onion, cilantro, lime juice and salt to taste. Stir well and serve.

1 quart

---

3 garlic cloves, minced or crushed
½ cup olive oil
12 ripe plum or other tomatoes (about 3 pounds)
Salt and pepper to taste
½ cup minced herbs, a combo of basil, oregano and parsley

For smoothest texture, peel tomatoes first (see below). For a chunkier texture leave the peels, and chop the tomatoes roughly.

Sauté garlic in olive oil until soft and fragrant. Add tomatoes, salt and pepper. Bring to a simmer, stirring occasionally. Cover and reduce heat to low for 15 minutes. Add herbs and continue to simmer for another 5 minutes. If you used unpeeled tomatoes, purée the sauce, if desired, using a blender or food processor.

Note: To peel the tomatoes, boil a medium pan ¾ full of water. Carefully place one tomato in the water for a few seconds. When the skin gets very tight, take the tomato out and hold it under cold running water. As soon as the tomato is cool enough to handle, cut out the stem and carefully remove the skin. Repeat with remaining tomatoes.

1½ quarts

Mexican Eggplant Dip

This makes a great dip for tortilla chips or fresh vegetables.

Fresh Tomato Sauce

It's the flavor of summer. How many days in a row can you eat tomatoes?

Rosemary Dijon Vinaigrette

A full-favored vinaigrette especially good on grilled vegetables.

2 tablespoons extra-virgin olive oil
Salt and pepper to taste
1 small garlic clove, minced or pressed
2 teaspoons fresh lemon juice
1 teaspoon Dijon mustard
1 teaspoon fresh rosemary, finely chopped

Whisk ingredients together in a small bowl and serve.

2 servings

Amazing Kale Pesto

This surprisingly delicious pesto is great many ways: spread on toast, in sandwiches, mixed with white beans or stirred into soup.

1 pound kale, dinosaur (Tuscan) or other type
2 to 3 tablespoons salt
2 garlic cloves
½ cup or more extra-virgin olive oil

Wash the kale in a sinkful of water. Remove the tough central ribs and core.

Bring 4 to 5 quarts of water to a rolling boil. Add 2 to 3 tablespoons salt and the kale and cook for 10 to 15 minutes or until tender. Drain, refresh in cold water and squeeze to remove all excess moisture.

Purée the greens, garlic, virgin olive oil and salt to taste in the food processor to form a smooth stiff paste. If needed, you can thin it with a little water. Store in the refrigerator in a glass jar or bowl covered with a layer of olive oil, where it will keep for a few days.

2 cups

18

4 medium beets
1½ tablespoons grapeseed, corn or other neutral-flavored oil
2 tablespoons sherry vinegar
2 teaspoons ginger, minced
Salt and pepper to taste
3 or 4 chives, minced (optional)

Cook beets as desired, testing for tenderness by poking with a toothpick or skewer:

- 🌿 Preheat oven to 375°F. Wrap the beets individually or together in aluminum foil. Bake until tender, from 1 to 1½ hours.

  OR

- 🌿 In a saucepan, cover beets with water, bring to a boil and cook until tender, from 30 to 45 minutes.

Cool. Rub the skins off the beets and cut them into cubes or strips, or, if you have a mandolin slicer, cut them into julienne.

Mix together the oil, vinegar, ginger, salt and pepper to taste in a bowl, then toss with the beets. Allow to rest for about 30 minutes before serving, if you have the time. Garnish with chives, if desired, and serve.

4 to 6 servings

2 bunches of medium or large beets, with beet greens
⅓ cup walnut oil
3 tablespoons fresh lemon juice
Salt and pepper to taste

Beets and Greens Salad

Wonderful for a nice bunch of garden-fresh beets.

Preheat the oven to 400°F. Cut the leafy greens and stems off the beets and save them.

See above to cook beets. Cool. Rub the skins off the beets and cut them into ½-inch dice.

While the beets are roasting, bring a large pot of salted water to a boil. Wash the beet greens well and break them into large pieces. Add the greens to the pot and cook 5 minutes or until tender. Drain well. Let cool, squeeze out excess water slice squeezed ball into ½-inch ribbons. Toss greens and beets with oil and lemon juice. Add salt and pepper to taste. Serve greens on a platter, scattered with cooked beet dice.

4 to 6 servings

Broccoli Potato Salad

An ideal summer pairing.

4 cups broccoli florets and peeled stems cut in bite-size pieces
4 to 5 thin-skinned potatoes (red-skinned or Yukon Gold)
¼ cup red wine vinegar
¼ cup honey
1 garlic clove, minced
¾ cup red onion, thinly sliced
1 tablespoon olive oil
5 cups tender greens, torn into bite-size pieces
Salt and pepper

Whisk vinegar, honey, and garlic in large bowl to blend. Season to taste with salt and pepper. Add red onion to dressing. Let stand while to soften onions while you cook the potatoes and broccoli,.

Steam broccoli until just tender, about 4 minutes. Rinse under cold water; drain.

Slice the potatoes into ¼-inch slices. Place in a saucepan of cold water with 1 tablespoon of salt. Cover and bring to a boil, until potatoes are just tender, about 5 minutes. Drain.

Whisk oil into the vinegar mixture. Gently stir into warm potatoes. Add broccoli and greens to potato mixture and toss gently to coat. Season with salt and pepper and serve.

6 servings

Moroccan Carrot Salad

Spicy and awesome— great for picnics.

1 pound carrots
¼ teaspoon turmeric
¼ teaspoon cumin, ground
1 red onion, minced
1 clove garlic, minced or pressed
1 tablespoon olive oil (add more as needed)
3 tablespoons chopped parsley
3 tablespoons of lemon juice
Salt and pepper to taste

Wash, peel and cut the carrots into thin slices. Steam until just tender. Drain and set aside.

Heat a medium skillet over moderate heat and toss in the turmeric and cumin. Toast until fragrant. Add the olive oil and sauté the onion and garlic over low heat until soft (add a little more olive oil if needed). Add the turmeric, cumin, parsley and lemon. Stir over heat until aromatic, about 20 seconds. Toss over the carrots, season with salt and pepper and set aside for at least 1 hour for the flavors to blend. Serve.

4 servings

3 large or 6 medium cucumbers
1 sweet red, yellow or orange pepper, seeded
½ jalapeño or other hot pepper, minced
2 teaspoons toasted sesame oil
1 tablespoon rice vinegar
1 teaspoon sugar, maple syrup or honey
dash of soy sauce

Peel cucumbers if the skins are tough and cut into halves lengthwise. Scoop out the seeds with a spoon, and cut each half into ½-inch slices.

Cut pepper into 1- to 2-inch long strips.

Toss cucumbers, peppers and jalapeño in a bowl.

Whisk together remaining ingredients and combine with cucumber mixture. Let sit at least 30 minutes before serving.

4 servings

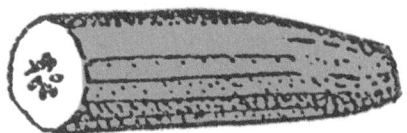

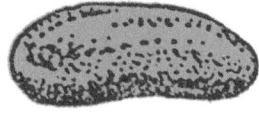

Sesame Cucumber Salad

Sesame adds presence to juicy summer vegetables.

4 large or 8 medium cucumbers
Salt and pepper to taste
⅓ cup white wine vinegar
½ large onion, sliced thinly
2 teaspoons sweet paprika
1 tablespoon minced fresh dill or 1 teaspoon dried
1½ teaspoon sugar
Pinch of hot paprika (optional)

Peel the cucumbers if necessary, leaving thin green stripes if desired, cut them in half lengthwise, and seed them with a spoon. Slice them thinly, toss with a generous amount of salt and leave to drain in a colander for 30 minutes.

In a medium bowl, combine the vinegar, onion slices, paprika, dill, sugar and pepper. Stir well and put aside for 30 minutes.

Give the cucumbers a quick rinse and spin or pat dry with a tea towel. Add them to the bowl of dressing and toss until all the slices are evenly coated. Taste and correct the seasoning if necessary. Let sit for at least 20 minutes and stir again before serving.

6 to 8 servings

Paprika Cucumber Salad

Opposites attract! Juicy, light cukes and spicy, sweet paprika are fantastic together!

Kohlrabi Salad

Kohlrabi are tender no matter how big they get.

3 medium (4-inch) kohlrabis, or equivalent
½ small red onion
1 tablespoon fresh lemon juice
Salt and pepper to taste
3 tablespoons olive oil
2 tablespoons drained capers
2 ounces small tender lettuce

Peel the kohlrabi and slice very thinly using a knife, food processor, slicing mandolin or the blade side of a box grater. Put the slices in a bowl.

Slice onion very thin, then rinse in a sieve and spin or pat dry. Stir into kohlrabi.

Stir together lemon juice, salt and pepper, then stir in oil and capers. Pour over kohlrabi. Toss with lettuce, then serve immediately.

6 to 8 servings

Famous Potato Salad

An adaptation of Cook's Illustrated's *killer potato salad—their recipes are so well-composed and well-tested that there's really no improving them; however, I've added our own little twists and shortcuts.*

2 pounds waxy potatoes, cut into ½-inch slices
2 tablespoons salt
1 medium clove garlic, minced
1½ tablespoons white wine vinegar
2 teaspoons Dijon mustard
¼ cup olive oil
½ teaspoon black pepper
1 small shallot or onion, minced (about 2 tablespoons)
4 tablespoons total minced fresh parsley, marjoram, chives basil

Place potatoes in large saucepan, cover with cold water, add salt. Bring to boil, then reduce heat to medium. Simmer potatoes, uncovered, until tender but still firm, about 5 minutes. Drain potatoes, setting aside ¼ cup of the cooking water.

Whisk garlic, potato cooking water, vinegar, mustard, oil and pepper in small bowl until combined. Drizzle dressing over warm potatoes; let stand 10 minutes.

Toss shallot or onion and herbs in small bowl. Drain extra dressing from the potatoes; add herb mixture and mix gently with rubber spatula.

6 servings

1 medium watermelon
4 tablespoons fresh mint, chopped
1 cup crumbled feta

Cut watermelon into 1-inch cubes, removing any seeds as needed. Transfer to serving bowl. Cover and refrigerate until chilled, at least 1 hour and up to 12 hours.

When ready to serve, add the mint and feta and toss again. Serve immediately.

6 to 8 servings

Watermelon Mint Salad with Feta

The great Rozanne Gold's amazing combination makes a wonderfully refreshing salad.

2 cucumbers
1 quart buttermilk
1 pint sour cream or Greek-style yogurt
⅓ cup lemon juice
1 teaspoon salt
4 teaspoons fresh dill, chopped
¼ cup parsley, chopped
4 scallions, white and pale green parts chopped

Peel the cucumbers, cut in half lengthwise, seed with a spoon, and roughly chop.

With a blender, purée the cucumbers and buttermilk until smooth. Add remaining ingredients; blend. Chill several hours, or overnight. The flavor develops over time.

6 servings

Chilled Cucumber Soup

No cooking for this cooling summertime treat.

Creamy Gazpacho

Adding bread to a cold soup may seem weird, but it's traditional and it works. Another secret—the flavor of tomatoes is amped up if you salt them ahead of time—it's a magic molecular thing. I do it whenever I use raw tomatoes.

3 pounds (about 6 medium) tomatoes
1 medium cucumber, peeled if necessary
1 medium bell pepper of any color, halved and cored
1 small onion, peeled
1 hot pepper, halved and cored if desired
1 garlic clove, chopped
3 slices of day-old bread, crusts removed
⅓ cup olive oil
3 tablespoons of vinegar, sherry vinegar is good
Salt and pepper to taste
Minced fresh herbs: parsley, basil, chives, tarragon, etc.

Roughly chop the tomatoes, cucumber, bell pepper and the onion and place in large bowl with the garlic, hot pepper and 1½ teaspoons salt. oss until well combined. Set aside for 30 minutes, if possible, to develop amazing flavors.

Add bread, torn into small pieces. Using a stick or countertop blender, purée mixture until smooth. With blender running, slowly drizzle in oil and continue to blend until completely emulsified, about 2 minutes.

Stir vinegar, season with salt and pepper. Cover and refrigerate for at least 2 hours to chill. Serve, topped with minced herbs and a drizzle of olive oil.

4 to 6 servings

Kernels cut from 5 ears of sweet corn
2 tablespoons olive oil
1 clove garlic, crushed
½ onion, chopped
1 jalapeño pepper, stemmed and chopped
Salt and black pepper
1½ cups vegetable or chicken broth

Combine the oil and the garlic in a saucepan over medium heat. Add the onion and jalapeño. Season with salt and pepper and sauté until the vegetables are soft and translucent, about 6 minutes. Use a blender to purée mixture together with corn, stirring as necessary.

Pour the purée into the saucepan and place over medium heat. Stir constantly for a few minutes, until the soup begins to simmer. Slowly stir in the chicken broth. Bring to a boil, decrease the heat to a simmer, cover, and cook for 15 minutes.

4 servings

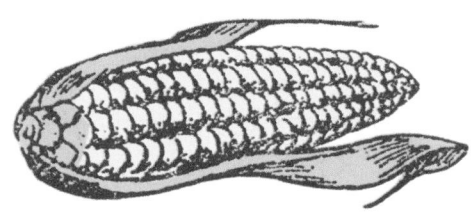

2 to 3 potatoes, peeled and sliced ½-inch thick
1 pound fresh spinach, trimmed
5 tablespoons unsalted butter
1 teaspoon salt, pepper to taste

In a large pot, add salt to 2 quarts of water and bring to a boil. Add the potatoes and cook over medium-high heat for 20 minutes.

Add the spinach and cook 10 more minutes. Do not overcook, or the spinach will turn dull.

Saving the broth, transfer the spinach and potatoes to a food processor or blender with a slotted spoon. If you've got a stick blender, dip out and save a cup or two of broth.

Blend until very smooth, adding the butter 1 tablespoon at a time. Put the purée back in the pot, if needed, and add the broth a bit at a time until you reach a consistency you like. Reheat gently, salt and pepper to taste. Serve hot.

6 servings

Fresh Sweet Corn Soup

Serve this with a dollop of fresh salsa or guacamole.

Creamy Spinach Soup

An amazingly delicious soup is adapted from one of Rozanne Gold's three-ingredient recipes And no cream!

Pan-Roasted Broccoli or Cauliflower

A nice, basic, one-pan recipe that works for any similar vegetable.

3 tablespoons water
Salt and pepper to taste
2 tablespoons vegetable oil
1 ¾ pounds broccoli or cauliflower

Wash the vegetables and cut the florets from the stems in bite-sized pieces. Peel the stems where the skin is fibrous and cut into floret sized pieces; keep separate.

In a 12-inch nonstick skillet with tight-fitting lid heat oil over medium-high heat until just beginning to smoke. Add stems in even layers and cook, without stirring, until browned on bottom, about 2 minutes. Add florets to skillet and toss to combine. Cook without stirring, until bottoms of florets just begin to brown, 1 to 2 minutes longer. Salt and pepper the vegetables.

Pour the water over the vegetables and cover the skillet; cook until tender-crisp, about 2 minutes. Uncover and continue to cook until water has evaporated, stems are tender and florets are tender-crisp, about 2 minutes more, and serve.

4 to 6 servings

Cauliflower and Chickpea Curry

Yummy!

2 tablespoons vegetable oil
2½ cups onions, chopped
5 teaspoons curry powder
6 cauliflower florets (about ⅓ medium head)
2 15-ounce cans garbanzo beans (chickpeas), drained
3 or 4 tomatoes, diced
2 fresh chile peppers, minced
14-ounce can unsweetened coconut milk
Salt and pepper to taste
½ cup fresh cilantro, chopped

Heat oil in large skillet over high heat. Add onions and sauté until golden brown, about 8 minutes. Add curry powder and stir 20 seconds. Add cauliflower and garbanzo beans; stir 1 minute. Add diced tomatoes with chiles, then coconut milk; bring to boil. Reduce heat to medium-low, cover and simmer gently until cauliflower is tender and liquid thickens slightly, stirring occasionally, about 15 minutes. Season to taste with salt and pepper. Stir in cilantro; serve.

6 servings

1 pound broccoli tops, separated into florets (save stems for soup)
3 tablespoons neutral-flavored oil
¾ cup fresh, coarse bread crumbs
1 teaspoon cardamom, ground
1 teaspoon salt
1 cup plain yogurt, room temperature

Cook the broccoli in a steamer until it is bright green and just tender, about 7 minutes. Drain, rinse in cold water and let dry in a colander or spin.

Meanwhile, place the oil in a 10-inch skillet over medium heat. A minute later, add the bread crumbs and increase the heat to high. Cook, stirring or shaking the pan until the crumbs brown, just a little over a minute. Drain the crumbs quickly in a strainer, then cool on paper towels remove as much of the remaining oil as possible. Combine the crumbs, cardamom and 1 teaspoon salt.

To serve, place a portion of broccoli on each plate with a spoonful of yogurt and a portion of the bread crumbs. To eat, dip the broccoli into the yogurt, then into the bread crumbs.

4 servings

Dip 'n' Eat Broccoli

Five-star food that a kid will love—this playful recipe is adapted from one by chef Jean-Georges Vongerichen. Spicy, salty, toasted crumbs— what's not to like?

4 teaspoons vegetable oil
¾ teaspoon chili powder
¼ cup mayonnaise
3 tablespoons sour cream
3 tablespoons fresh cilantro, minced
1 medium clove of garlic, minced or pressed
½ teaspoon cayenne pepper
pinch salt
4 teaspoons lime juice
½ cup grated Parmesan cheese
6 large ears of corn, shucked

Get your grill going and oil the grate.

While the grill is heating, mix the vegetable oil, salt and ¼ teaspoon of the chili powder and rub down the ears.

Mix the rest of the ingredients in a large bowl and set aside. Grill the corn over hot coals, turning until lightly charred on all sides, 7 to 12 minutes. Remove from grill and slather with mayo mixture.

6 servings

Mexican Grilled Sweet Corn

Since the ancient Mexicans invented corn, they've had eons to hone this amazing dish that dreams are made of.

Blackened String Beans

These fabulous, spicy string beans are an adaptation of ones they serve at New World Home Cooking in Saugerties, NY.

2 pounds fresh string beans, stem ends trimmed
2 tablespoons vegetable oil (not olive oil)
1½ teaspoons cayenne pepper
4 teaspoons chili powder
3 teaspoons cornmeal
2 teaspoons dried herbs: oregano, basil, marjoram or thyme
2 teaspoons salt
1 tablespoon ground black pepper
1 tablespoon garlic powder or combination garlic and onion powder (not granules)

In a steamer, cook beans until crisp-tender. Refresh in cold water and spin or let dry.

In a bowl, mix the beans with the oil. Mix the remaining ingredients together and then add them to coat the beans.

Open your windows, turn on the fan, heat a large skillet on high. Alternatively, use a grill and grill basket. Toss the beans in small batches until the spices are charred, serve with lemon wedges.

6 servings

Peppers 'n' Onions

A terrific, easy, vegetable dish to serve with meat, fish, or other veggies. The leftovers are delicious on sandwiches or in wraps.

1 sweet pepper (any color) per serving, cored and sliced
1 medium onion per serving, peeled and sliced
½ garlic clove per serving, minced
2 teaspoons olive or other vegetable oil per serving
Salt and pepper to taste
Optional: fresh basil, parsley or other herbs, finely chopped
Optional: fresh hot peppers, cored and minced

Heat the oil over medium-high heat, add the pepper, onions and garlic. Cook and stir until limp and beginning to become brown. Add salt, black pepper and herbs to taste, and stir again.

2 servings

1 pound mustard greens, collard greens or kale
¾ cup sugar or maple syrup
½ cup vinegar
1 tablespoon salt
1 teaspoon whole blackpeppercorns

Wash, dry, and coarsely chop the greens, including stems. In a large pot, combine 2 cups water, the sugar or syrup, the vinegar, salt and peppercorns. Bring to a boil, lower the heat and cook 5 minutes.

Add the greens to the pot. Cook 2 minutes and let cool. Transfer to a bowl or jar, cover and let sit 2 days, refrigerated, before using.

4 to 6 servings

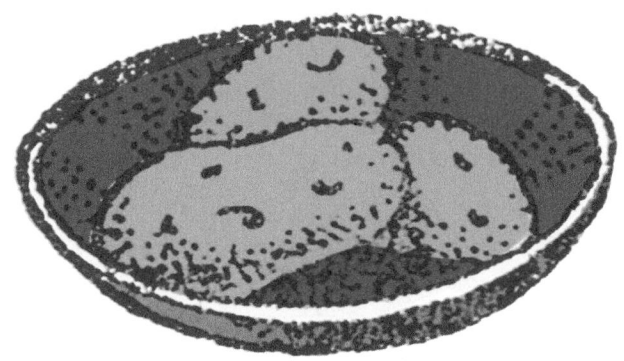

5 medium potatoes, peeled and cut into 1-inch chunks
1 tablespoon salt
6 tablespoons butter, melted and cooled
⅔ cup room-temperature buttermilk
Pepper to taste

Place potatoes in large saucepan; add cold water to cover by 1 inch and add salt. Bring to boil over high heat, then reduce heat to medium and simmer until potatoes are just cooked, about 18 minutes. Drain potatoes and return to saucepan set on still-hot burner.

Using potato masher, mash potatoes. Slowly whisk melted butter into room-temperature buttermilk in small bowl until combined. Then gently fold buttermilk mixture into the potatoes. Adjust seasoning with salt and pepper; serve immediately.

4 servings

Pickled Greens

If you've got more greens than you can eat, this is a good way to preserve them, and they're great on sandwiches.

Buttermilk Mashed Potatoes

Baked Summer Squash Mélange

There are so many fun types and shapes of squash in the summer— here's a way to taste test them together. Sub other fresh herbs if you like.

About 10 small (5 to 6-inch) summer squash: zucchini, pattypan, crook-neck, straight neck, etc.
3 small onions
3 medium garlic cloves, sliced
1 teaspoon fresh rosemary, minced
1 teaspoon fresh oregano , minced
Salt and pepper to taste
⅓ cup olive oil
1 tablespoon red wine vinegar
Fresh tender green herbs: parsley, basil or mint, tiny leaves or chopped

Preheat oven to 400°F. Cut squash into bite-size slices or wedges; there should be about 5 or 6 cups. Peel onions, slice them and separate into rings.

Oil a large baking dish and spread the squash evenly in it. Sprinkle with the garlic, rosemary, oregano, pepper and salt. Drizzle with oil and sprinkle with vinegar. Cover tightly with foil or lid.

Bake in upper level of oven 20 minutes. Uncover and toss. Continue baking until squash is just barely tender, 5 to 10 minutes. Do not cook until soft, because the mixture will continue to cook after removed from oven.

Serve warm or room temperature. Garnish with fresh herbs.

6 servings

Herbed Zucchini Coins

Sub any kind of summer squash for zukes.

2 tablespoons olive oil
1 tablespoon unsalted butter
2 pounds small zucchini, cut into ½-inch thick rounds
¼ cup white wine vinegar
Salt and pepper to taste
1 to 2 tablespoons fresh mint or other green herb, chopped

Heat oil and butter in a large heavy skillet over medium-high heat until foam subsides, then cook zucchini, stirring occasionally, allowing each side to turn golden brown.

Add vinegar and salt and cook, shaking skillet, until vinegar has evaporated. Remove from heat and toss in mint. Add pepper and toss.

6 servings

**Herbed
Spaghetti
Squash
with
Peppers
and
Walnuts**

1 spaghetti squash (about 2 pounds)
2 medium red or green bell peppers
3 tablespoons olive oil
1 teaspoon minced or pressed garlic
Salt and pepper to taste
1 teaspoon wine vinegar
½ cup pan-toasted walnuts, coarsely chopped
¼ cup slivered cilantro or basil leaves

Cut the spaghetti squash in half lengthwise and cook it, using one of the following methods:

- 🌿 Bake cut-side down in a baking pan about 35 minutes at 375°F.

- 🌿 Microwave 6 to 8 minutes (let stand for a few minutes afterwards).

- 🌿 Boil 20 minutes or so until tender inside (outside remains crisp).

Meanwhile, remove the stems and cores of the peppers, then slice as thinly as possible (use a slicing mandolin or food processor, if desired).

Warm the oil in medium skillet over moderate heat. Sauté peppers until just slightly softened. Add garlic, salt and pepper and stir a minute. Add vinegar and set aside.

Cool squash briefly. Scoop out seeds. Gently comb out all strands with a fork, fluffing into a serving dish.

Add pepper mixture to squash, tossing to blend well. Add the walnuts and cilantro and toss to mix. Serve hot, warm or at room temperature.

4 to 6 servings as a side dish

My favorite spaghetti squash recipe—just enough heft to feel satisfying. A good picnic dish.

Marinated Vegetables a la Grecque

Great for cooking whatever vegetables are fresh with any seasonal herbs. They also make a beautiful platter.

Several cups of prepped vegetables (see below)
2 cups white wine
2/3 cup olive oil
1 teaspoon salt
10 to 12 peppercorns
1 bay leaf
1 tablespoon fresh herbs of your choice or 1 teaspoon dried
2 or 3 garlic cloves, peeled
Optional: onion, lemon juice, vinegar (if desired)

Clean and trim each vegetable, cut them into serving-size pieces. You'll cook them in separate batches, the most delicate first.

Combine the rest of the ingredients (except the optional ones) in a large skillet with the first batch of vegetables. Add just enough water to cover whatever vegetable is being cooked. Simmer the vegetable until it is just barely tender. Using a slotted spoon, lift them out, blot the oil off and arrange on platter.

Cook the next groups of vegetables in the same way. Add optional ingredients as desired to the marinating liquid to flavor vegetables.

The platters can be decorated with sprigs of herbs and/or thinly sliced lemons and chilled until serving.

32

12 to 16 zucchini or other squash flowers (male or female)
2 eggs
1 cup cold water
1 cup flour
Salt and pepper to taste
Vegetable oil for frying (sunflower, corn or peanut)

Open up the blossoms and remove the reproductive parts. Cut the stems to within an inch of the blossom or baby squash forming in the stem. Mix together the eggs, water and flour with a whisk until blended.

Heat ½" of oil in a skillet until a drop of batter sizzles and floats to the top. Dip each flower in the batter and then cook about 1 minute on each side until golden brown. Drain on paper-towel lined plate. Serve immediately. Delicious with salsa or Sriracha (chili-garlic) sauce.

Before frying, you can stuff the flowers with cheese or other filling. Adjust cooking time accordingly.

6 appetizer servings

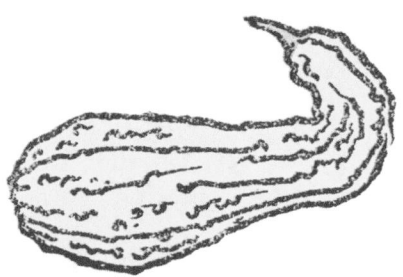

1 clove garlic, minced or pressed
½ teaspoon or so of crushed red pepper flakes
½ cup black olives, pitted and roughly chopped
¼ cup plus 1 tablespoon olive oil
1 pound spaghetti, linguini or other pasta
1 pound spinach, washed, tough stems removed, chopped
Salt and pepper to taste
Grated Parmesan cheese, if desired

Bring a large pot of water to a boil and add a tablespoon of salt. Meanwhile combine garlic in the bottom of a warm bowl with the red pepper flakes, olives and oil.

Place the pasta in the pot, and cook until nearly done. Plunge the spinach into the water and cook until it wilts, less than a minute. Drain quickly, allowing some water to cling to the pasta, and toss pasta and spinach in the bowl with the garlic and olive mixture. Season with salt and pepper and serve, passing the cheese.

3 to 4 servings

Concord Grape Sorbet

It's the grapiest! Sugar and alcohol keep sorbet and ice cream from freezing rock hard, so don't scrimp.

4 pounds Concord grapes, stems removed
1 cup (or more) water
¾ cup sugar
1 tablespoon vodka

Combine grapes and 1 cup water in heavy large saucepan. Bring to boil. Reduce heat, cover and simmer until grapes are very tender, about 15 minutes. Transfer grape mixture to strainer. Set over large bowl. Using spoon, press on grapes to extract as much liquid as possible. Measure liquid; add water if necessary to make 4 cups. Add sugar and vodka; stir until dissolved. Pour mixture into an ice cream maker and process according to manufacturers instructions. Freeze until firm, about 2 hours.

1 quart

Fresh Berry Kir Imperial

A great way to celebrate berry season.

3 cups fresh ripe raspberries or more for garnish (optional)
1 bottle sparkling wine or champagne, chilled
1½ cups fresh blueberries and more for garnish (optional)

Put 8 champagne flutes or wine glasses in the freezer.

With a countertop or stick blender, purée 1½ cups of the raspberries and 6 tablespoons of the champagne until very smooth.

Remove the glasses from the freezer. In each glass, put 3 tablespoons raspberries and 3 tablespoons blueberries and pour some raspberry purée over the berries. Fill the glass to the top with champagne. Garnish with extra berries, if desired.

8 servings

34

1 cup all-purpose flour
½ teaspoon baking powder
½ teaspoon baking soda
¼ teaspoon salt
½ stick unsalted butter, softened
2/3 cup sugar
½ teaspoon pure vanilla extract
1 large egg
½ cup buttermilk or yogurt
1 cup fresh raspberries
1½ tablespoons sugar

Raspberry Buttermilk Cake

This cake is stupendous with any fresh fruit — blueberries, sliced peaches, or whatever is in season!

Preheat oven to 400°F with rack in middle. Butter a 9-inch round cake pan and sprinkle with flour, tapping to coat evenly.

In a medium bowl, whisk together flour, baking powder, baking soda and salt.

In a large bowl with an electric mixer, beat butter and sugar until pale and fluffy, about 2 minutes, then beat in vanilla. Add egg and beat well.

At low speed, mix in flour mixture in 3 batches, alternating with buttermilk or yogurt, beginning and ending with flour, mixing until just combined.

Spoon batter into cake pan, smoothing top. Scatter raspberries evenly over top and sprinkle with 1½ tablespoons sugar.

Bake until a wooden pick inserted into center comes out clean, 25 to 30 minutes. Cool in pan 10 minutes, then turn out onto a rack to finish cooling. Invert onto a plate to serve.

8 servings

2½ cups of fruit: peaches, berries, plums, other fresh seasonal fruit
½ cup white grape juice or orange juice
Sugar or maple syrup (optional)

Fruit Ice Pops

Your kids will always remember these.

Purée the fruit with a blender or food processor, mix with juice and taste for sweetness. Add sugar or syrup, if desired. Pour into ice pop molds, or use small paper cups with a wooden stick or spoon propped through slitted paper or foil and freeze until solid.

4 pops

Soup of Red Fruits

Any red, purple, or blue fruits that are in season can be featured in this dessert soup.

½ pound cherries, pits removed and reserved
½ cup sugar or maple syrup
2 cups strawberries, cored and halved (or quartered if very large)
1 cup blueberries
1 cup raspberries
3 tablespoons lemon juice
Mint leaves

Crack the cherry pits by smacking them lightly with a hammer or the bottom of a saucepan; don't pulverize them, just expose their centers. Place them in a saucepan with sugar or syrup and 1 cup water. Bring to a boil over high heat. Reduce the heat to medium and cook for 5 minutes. Remove from the heat and cool slightly.

Strain and return the liquid to the saucepan. Add the cherries and cook over medium heat until they are tender, 10 to 15 minutes. Cool, then chill. Place the berries in a bowl and pour the cherries and their juices over them. Add the lemon juice, garnish with mint leaves and serve immediately with shortbread cookies, or refrigerate for up to a day.

6 servings

Autumn

Early autumn in the Hudson Valley is the most abundant season for locavores! The great summer veggies are still rolling in, plus later crops like winter squash, potatoes, Brussels sprouts, onions and garlic. As the days get cooler, our appetite for heartier food matches the ripening crops. The sheer abundance at farmstands and farmers markets can be a bit overwhelming, so take it slow, cruise around before you buy anything and check out all the varieties. Then go through a second time to fill your market basket.

I love collecting a variety of winter squash—from the buff-colored butternut, to the big bluish-green hubbards, the bright orange kabochas and the wildly spattered carnival acorn squash. At home I pile them in a bowl or basket and they're a big, dramatic decoration. If kept cool and dry, winter squash will miraculously stay good and edible until spring, if you can bear watching your arrangement disappear bit by bit.

The hearty flavors of the kale and cabbage family are said to improve after a frost or two, which slows their growth and sweetens even brussels sprouts, which some find too bitter earlier in the season.

Apples are a wonderful local specialty and you will be amazed to find dozens of varieties of apples grown here, with romantic, exotic names like Northern Spy, Golden Russet, Winesap, and even Lady Sweet. Fresh local cider is just extraordinary, and now there are lots of local breweries producing hard cider, a great beer alternative. Grapes, raspberries and pumpkins round out the plentiful fruit choices.

Cauliflower Salad with Raisins and Pine Nuts

Delicious sweet-tart salad to serve warm or room temperature. Sub broccoli if you'd like.

1 medium white, green, gold or purple cauliflower
2 tablespoons pine nuts
¼ cup golden or black raisins
¼ cup fruit vinegar
¼ cup onion, diced
Salt and pepper to taste
1½ tablespoons olive oil
2 teaspoons capers or chopped pickles
½ teaspoon cornstarch
2 tablespoons water

Trim the large leaves and peel the base of the cauliflower. Cut it shaking the pot once or twice to cook the vegetables evenly.

Meanwhile, toast pine nuts, stirring, in a small heavy pan over fairly low heat until golden—keep an eye on these, they burn quickly and they're wicked expensive. Spread out to cool. In the same pan, combine raisins, vinegar, onion, salt, pepper, oil and capers. Cover and bring to a simmer over low heat. Stir together cornstarch and water. Add to pan, stirring constantly until mixture thickens and turns clear. Remove from heat. Pour over the cauliflower. Serve warm.

4 to 6 servings

Roasted Squash and Potatoes with Rosemary

A fragrant, warming dish to serve when the leaves turn colors. All kinds of winter squash are yummy!

2 yellow-fleshed or other potatoes, peeled if desired, and cut into ¾-inch cubes, about 2 cups
1 medium winter squash, peeled and cut into 1-inch cubes, about 4 cups
¼ olive oil
2 tablespoons fresh sage, rosemary, marjoram or savory
Salt and pepper to taste

Preheat the oven to 400°F.

Place the potatoes and squash in one layer in a nonstick roasting pan. Drizzle with oil, sprinkle with herbs and season with salt and pepper.

Roast the potatoes and squash, stirring after 30 minutes to cook evenly, for 1 hour or until well browned. Serve hot or warm.

4 to 6 servings

Cauliflower Salad with Olives and Bread Crumbs

Italians have wonderful ways with cauliflower. This dish is both simple and surprising.

1 medium white, green, gold or purple cauliflower
½ small red onion, very thinly sliced
½ cup oil-cured black olives, pitted and coarsely chopped
¼ cup extra-virgin olive oil
2 tablespoons red wine vinegar
Salt and pepper to taste
1 cup bread crumbs
¼ cup parsley leaves, minced

Trim the large leaves and peel the base of the cauliflower. Cut it into florets and bite-sized pieces. Steam until crisp-tender in a basket over boiling water, shaking the pot once or twice to cook the vegetable evenly.

Meanwhile, in a medium skillet over medium-high heat, warm about half the oil, then add the bread crumbs and toast until brown. Spread over a paper towel to cool.

Put the steamed cauliflower in a medium bowl along with the onion and olives. Drizzle with the rest of the oil and all the vinegar and sprinkle with salt and lots of pepper. Toss and set aside.

Mix the bread crumbs with the parsley and sprinkle the cauliflower with half of the crumb mixture. Pass the rest at the table.

4 servings

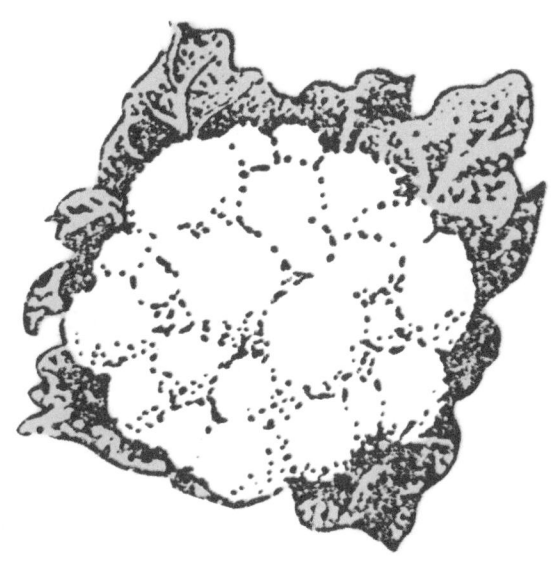

Savory Grain and Winter Squash Bake

A party in a casserole—a fantastic potluck dish. Also good for a harvest dinner.

¼ cup olive oil
¾ cup millet, quinoa, farro or cracked wheat
1 medium winter squash or 1 small pumpkin, peeled, seeded and cut into 1-inch cubes
1 cup fresh or dried cranberries
Salt and pepper to taste
1 tablespoon minced fresh sage, savory or thyme leaves or 1 teaspoon dried
2 tablespoons maple syrup or honey (none if using dried cranberries)
1 cup vegetable stock or water, warmed
¼ cup pumpkin seeds or coarsely chopped nuts

Preheat the oven to 375°F and grease a 2-quart casserole, a 9 x 13" or other large baking dish with oil.

Put 2 tablespoons of the oil in a small skillet over medium-high heat. When hot, add the grain and cook, stirring frequently, until fragrant and toasted, about 3 minutes. Spread on the bottom of the baking dish.

Scatter the squash or pumpkin cubes and the cranberries on top of the grain. Sprinkle with the herbs, salt and pepper and drizzle with syrup, if using. Pour the warmed stock in carefully. Cover tightly with lid or foil and bake, without stirring, for 45 minutes.

Uncover and turn the oven up to 400°F. Take a taste and adjust the seasonings. If it looks dry, add a couple of spoonsful of water or stock. Sprinkle the seeds or nuts on top and return the dish to the oven. Bake until the mixture bubbles and the top is browned—another 10 minutes or so. Serve hot or at room temperature.

4 to 6 servings

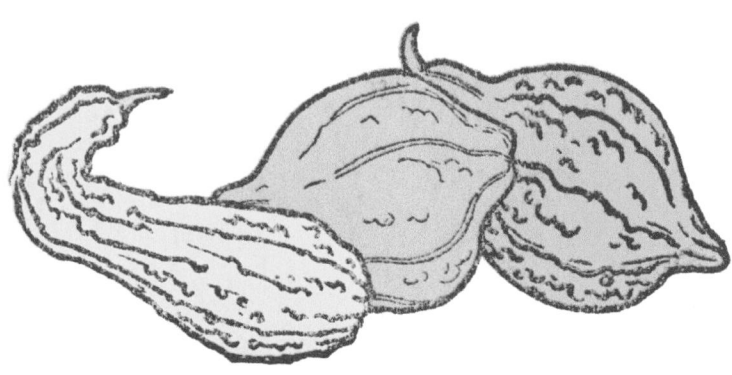

2 pounds winter squash
1 orange
2 tablespoons unsalted butter
Salt and pepper

Preheat the oven to 400°F. Cut the squash in half lengthwise. Remove seeds and any membrane. Place in baking pan flesh side down and pour ¼ cup water over the top. Bake for 1 hour, turning over after 30 minutes. Squash will be lightly caramelized.

Remove the flesh from the skin, purée until smooth with a food processor, an electric mixer or a potato masher. Add 2 teaspoons grated orange zest and 2 tablespoons fresh orange juice. Cut the butter into small pieces and mix it in. Add salt and pepper to taste.

4 to 5 servings

Sunny Winter Squash & Orange Purée

A magic combination—this tastes and looks like autumn sunshine.

---

1 acorn, butternut or other winter squash
2 tablespoons cream
2 tablespoons maple syrup

Preheat oven to 350°F.

Cut squash into halves. Remove seeds and fibers with a spoon. Place squash, cut-sides up, in baking dish. Spoon maple syrup and cream into each half. Bake, uncovered, for 50 minutes.

4 servings

Maple Baked Squash

A simple and delicious dish that can be made entirely of local ingredients.

---

1 quart water
2 tablespoons kosher salt
2 cups pumpkin or winter squash seeds
1½ teaspoons vegetable oil

Preheat oven to 350°F. To separate seeds from fibers, put the whole mess in a bowl or clean sink of water and squeeze/squish with your hands (a good job for kids). Skim off floating seeds. Small seeds can be eaten whole, but large seeds have heavy hulls that must be cracked open and discarded.

Toss seeds with oil. Spread on a baking sheet or in a wide baking pan. Bake until golden and crisp, 20 to 40 minutes, tossing often.

2 cups

Roasted Pumpkin Seeds

What to do with your Jack-O-Lantern guts!

Orange Zesty Brussels Sprouts

A delicious Brussels sprouts dish that will make fans of foes.

2 cups medium-to-large Brussels sprouts
1 orange
1 tablespoon lemon juice
1 teaspoon honey
Salt and pepper to taste
big pinch of caraway seeds
2 scallions
1 tablespoon vegetable oil

Trim bases of sprouts and remove wilted leaves. Slice thickly by hand or using a food processor.

Grate or finely chop ½ teaspoon of zest from the orange and set it aside. Squeeze ½ cup of orange juice into a small bowl. Add lemon juice, honey, salt and pepper and mix.

Toast caraway seeds in a large heavy skillet over low heat, stirring until fragrant. Grind, smash or chop the seeds and set aside. Trim scallions and slice thin, adding the green part to the caraway and the white part to the orange zest.

Heat the oil in the same skillet over moderate heat. Add orange zest mixture, stir, then the sprouts, toss, cover and cook about 3 minutes. Add the juice mixture, toss, cover and cook just until wilted; start checking after a couple minutes. Remove the lid, raise the heat and allow the juices to reduce to a glaze.

Add scallion greens and caraway and toss.

2 servings

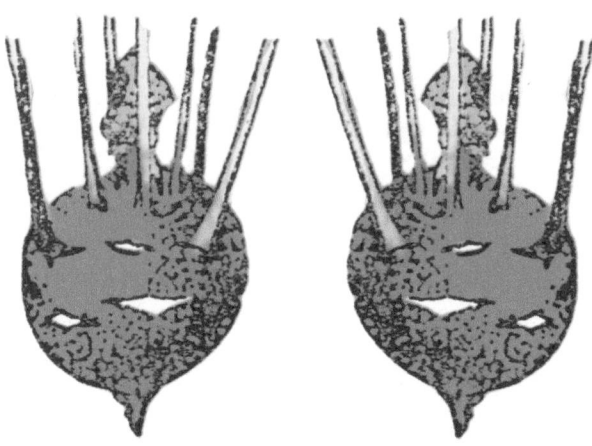

2 cups Brussels sprouts
1 tablespoon sesame seeds
1 teaspoon honey
Salt and pepper to taste
1 tablespoon dry sherry or vermouth
1 tablespoon peanut oil
1 tablespoon fresh ginger, minced

Fill a large pot with water, add a tablespoon of salt and bring to a boil. Meanwhile, trim the bases of Brussels sprouts and remove any yellowing or loose leaves. Halve the sprouts, or quarter them if they're big.

Drop them into boiling water and simmer until just tender throughout, about 4 minutes.

Meanwhile, in a heavy skillet over medium heat, stir sesame seeds until evenly tan, a minute or two.

Drain sprouts well. Stir together honey, salt, and sherry.

Heat the oil in the heavy skillet, add ginger and stir over moderate heat until lightly colored. Add sprouts and toss to coat. Add sherry mixture and toss gently.

Transfer to warm serving dish. Sprinkle with sesame seeds.

4 servings

Brussels Sprouts with Ginger and Sesame

A fun new spin on Brussels sprouts. Try this if you think you don't like them.

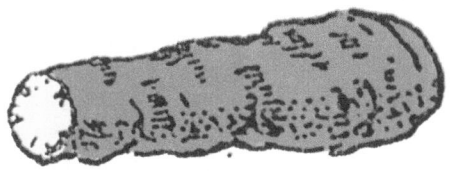

4 medium kohlrabis
2 tablespoons olive or vegetable oil or butter
1 small shallot, minced
Salt and pepper to taste

Remove kohlrabi leaves, if any. Peel kohlrabis thoroughly, removing any tough fibers. Halve the bulbs. Grate using hand grater or food processor.

Heat the oil or butter in wide skillet over moderate heat. Toss in the kohlrabi shreds and shallot over moderate heat until tender, a matter of a few minutes. Season with salt and pepper.

2 to 3 servings

Sauteed Kohlrabi Shreds

Here's a nice recipe for an underknown vegetable.

Herbed Brussels Sprouts Shreds with Toasted Nuts

Substitute vegetables, nuts and herbs at will.. Serve it over whole grain and it's a meal.

4 cups Brussels sprouts
¼ cup olive oil or 4 tablespoons (½ stick) of butter
Salt and pepper to taste
½ cup chopped hazelnuts or other nuts
1 tablespoon balsamic vinegar or lemon juice
¼ cup shredded fresh herbs: mint, dill or parsley leaves

Trim the stems from the Brussels sprouts, then cut each one into thin slices or shreds with a knife, grater, mandolin or food processor.

Put half the oil or butter in a large skillet over medium-high heat. When it's hot, add the sprouts and ¼ cup water; sprinkle with salt and pepper, turn the heat to medium and cover. Cook for about 5 minutes or until nearly tender.

Meanwhile, heat the remaining oil or butter in a small skillet over medium heat. Add the nuts and cook, stirring almost constantly until fragrant, about 5 minutes.

When the sprouts are nearly cooked, uncover and raise the heat a little. Cook until any remaining water evaporates and the sprouts are fully tender, another 5 to 10 minutes, stirring. Stir in the vinegar, garnish with the nuts and their butter or oil and the herbs, and serve.

4 servings

Potent Oven-dried Tomatoes

Tomatoes, technically a fruit, have lots of sugar and dry as nicely as other juicy fruits. These will be much fresher than store bought.

24 ripe plum tomatoes

Preheat the oven to 225°F. Set 2 wire racks on top of 2 baking sheets.

Cut the tomatoes in half lengthwise and scoop out the seeds with your fingers or a spoon (save and add to soup—the gel surrounding the seeds is the most umami part of the tomato). Put the tomatoes on the racks, cut-side down, in the oven for 2 hours.

Check on the tomatoes and rotate the sheets 180°.

If you want to store the tomatoes in a jar at room temperature, let them dry completely, 6 hours or more—they will be dark and crunchy,

If you prefer moister, softer tomatoes, shorten drying time, then either use the tomatoes immediately or store them in the freezer.

44

3 or 4 medium turnips
1 teaspoon salt
1 pound turnip greens, spinach or chard
2 tablespoons olive oil
1 large garlic clove, pressed or minced
Pinch of chili flakes
About 1 tablespoon sherry vinegar

Trim and rinse turnips. Slice into ¾-inch dice. Combine with salt in colander, tossing to coat. Let stand 15 minutes or more to release some water. Meanwhile, clean the greens in several changes of water. Discard the heaviest stems. Thinly slice the rest.

Rinse and spin or pat the cubes dry. Heat a large skillet with 1 tablespoon of oil over medium-high heat. Add turnips and toss until lightly browned (raise heat if needed), 8 to 10 minutes. Add garlic and chili flakes and sauté another minute.

Add the greens, toss, cover and cook about 2 minutes. Toss, re-cover, and cook until turnips are tender, 2 to 3 minutes longer. If there's a lot of juice, remove the cover, turn up the heat and boil away the extra.

Off heat or in a serving bowl, add the vinegar and the remaining tablespoon oil to the turnips and toss. Serve warm or at room temperature.

4 servings

Turnips with Greens and Garlic

If you have turnips with their greens, here's a dish with both. Super with rutabaga and spinach, or any root veggie and greens combo.

Zippy Collard Ribbons with Sesame Seeds

Quickly cooked collards are very different from traditional southern slow stewing.

2 pounds collard greens, approximately
1 tablespoon molasses
¾ teaspoon salt
1 tablespoon peanut oil
2 teaspoons Asian (dark) sesame oil
Pinch of chili flakes
1 garlic clove, minced
2 teaspoons sherry vinegar or cider vinegar
1½ tablespoons sesame seeds, toasted in a hot skillet

Strip the stems from leaves and discard. Rinse the leaves well. Stack them and slice into ¼-inch strips.

Combine them in very large, deep skillet with 2 cups of water, molasses, salt, peanut and sesame oils. Bring to a boil, stirring, until limp. Cover and simmer until the collards are tender but chewy, about 15 minutes.

Add the chili flakes and garlic. Remove the cover, raise heat and boil, stirring often, until the pot liquor has mostly evaporated, about 5 minutes.

Season with vinegar. Sprinkle with sesame seeds and serve hot.

4 servings

Braised Leeks

A lavish vegetable dish, naturally sweet and rich.

¼ cup olive oil or butter
3 or 4 leeks, about 1½ pounds, trimmed and cleaned
Salt and pepper to taste
½ cup vegetable stock or water
1 tablespoon lemon juice
Parsley leaves, chopped for garnish

Heat the oil or butter in a large skillet or saucepan over moderate heat. When the oil or butter is hot, add the leeks, arranging them in one layer. Sprinkle with salt and pepper and cook, turning once or twice until just beginning to brown, about 5 minutes.

Add the stock, bring to a boil. Turn the heat to low, cover; cook until the leeks are tender, about 20 minutes. Uncover; if needed, raise the heat and boil away some liquid, but keep moist.

Sprinkle about 1 tablespoon of lemon juice over the leeks, then taste and season. Serve hot, at room temperature or cold, sprinkled with a little lemon juice and garnished with parsley.

4 servings

2 tablespoons butter, peanut oil or other oil
2 cloves of garlic, minced or pressed
1 teaspoon fresh ginger, peeled and minced or grated
1 teaspoon salt
1 teaspoon pepper
½ teaspoon ground turmeric
¼ teaspoon cayenne
½ teaspoon ground cinnamon
Pinch freshly grated nutmeg
1 teaspoon ground coriander
1 teaspoon ground cumin
1 head cauliflower, about ½ pounds, trimmed and broken into florets
1 cup cored, seeded and chopped tomatoes (canned are okay, don't drain)
½ cup water
1½ cups optional vegetable, chopped into ½-inch dice
Minced cilantro leaves for garnish

In large, deep skillet add the oil or butter and turn the heat to medium. When hot, add the garlic and ginger. Cook, stirring until the garlic begins to color, about 5 minutes.

Add the salt and spices and cook, stirring for 30 seconds, or until the spices release their aromas. Add the cauliflower, tomatoes and water. Stir, cover, and turn the heat to medium-low. Cook, checking and stirring every few minutes until the cauliflower is almost tender, about 10 minutes.

Add the additional vegetables and adjust the seasoning. Cook until the cauliflower is tender, then garnish and serve with rice or other cooked grain.

4 servings

Braised Cauliflower with Curry and Tomatoes

This dish makes the most of the meatiness of cauliflower— if you don't know what I'm talking about, try this recipe. Substitute a tablespoon of curry powder for the spices if you're in a hurry.

Pasta with Beets, Greens and Pecans

You can use any color of beets here — traditional red ones will turn the pasta pink.

2 bunches small beets with nice, fresh greens
1 to 2 tablespoons vinegar, either fruit or red wine
½ pound small- to medium-sized pasta
2 tablespoons pecan, walnut, or olive oil
1 small garlic clove, minced or pressed
Pinch of chili flakes
Salt and pepper
¼ cup toasted pecans (or walnuts), coarsely chopped

Cut off beet greens 1 inch from the beet. Scrub the beets. Cook beets as desired (see page 4), Cool. Rub the skins off the beets and slice or quarter them. Toss with vinegar.

Wash the beet greens, removing wilted ones. Chop coarsely.

Cook pasta in large pot of boiling, salted water until almost tender. Drain, saving a large spoonful of pasta water.

Meanwhile, heat 1 tablespoon oil in large skillet over moderate heat. Add garlic and chili flakes and toss. Add greens, a tablespoon of water, toss and cover, stirring every couple of minutes until greens are wilted. Season with salt and pepper. Add pasta and spoonful of pasta water, stir and let cook together a few minutes.

Toss with remaining tablespoon of oil. Top with beets and nuts.

2 servings

6 cups sliced or chopped fruit (2 to 3 pounds), trimmed, peeled, pitted and cored as necessary
½ teaspoon ground cinnamon
½ cup brown sugar or a scant ½ cup white sugar with a spoon of molasses or ½ cup maple syrup
5 tablespoons cold butter, cut into bits
½ cup rolled oats
½ cup whole wheat flour
¼ cup chopped walnuts or pecans
Pinch salt

Heat the oven to 400°F. Spread the fruit out in a buttered or oiled 8-inch square or 9-inch round baking pan.

Combine the rest of the ingredients in the container of a food processor. Pulse a few times, then process until everything is well incorporated but not uniform. The mixture should be crumbly.

(To mix the ingredients by hand, toss together the dry ingredients, then work in softened butter with your fingers or a fork.)

Crumble the topping over the fruit and bake 30 to 40 minutes, until the topping is browned and the fruit is tender and bubbling. Serve hot, warm or at room tempereature.

8 servings

Fruit Crisp

It's easy to double the topping mix and freeze the extra.

---

4 cups water or 3 cups dry red or white wine and 1 cup water
4 pears, apples or quince
1 cup sugar or maple syrup
1 lemon

Mix the liquid with the sugar or syrup and bring to a boil. Turn down and add the juice and zest of the lemon.

Peel the fruit, leaving the stem if possible. Use a spoon or melon baller to scoop the core out of the blossom end, if desired. Place in the simmering liquid, adding water to cover. Cook from 15 to 40 minutes only until tender. Test with a small knife or pick.

You can remove the fruit, and then boil down the liquid over high heat and serve as a sauce, if you like.

4 servings

Poached Pears, Apples or Quince

A classic autumn dessert, great with cookies. Red wine will turn the fruit a lovely shade of burgundy.

Winter

Winter in the northeast may seem like a terrible time for local produce, and it's true that the choice is drastically diminished. But there's a surprisingly variety, nonetheless. Root vegetables lead the pack—and there are plenty that are so venerable they're new again. Parsnips look like a fat white carrot, and are a cousin. They don't fully ripen until after the weather's gotten cold. They've got the perfume of parsley, another relative and when roasted or boiled taste like parsley potatoes, but sweeter. Another relative of carrots is celeriac, or celery root, a big, knobby softball of a root with awesome celery flavor. And there are more—beets come in colors from signature magenta to brilliant golden yellow. Sunny rutabaga is another under-known, and delicious root. And of course there are all kinds of potatoes, white, red, yellow and blue. Cabbages keep in the cold well, and the purple variety has even more vitamins that standard green. And somehow dried beans are so good in the winter, and there are so many ways to serve them.

If you froze fruit in the summer, now's the time to enjoy a bit of summer sun in the middle of the cold. Local apples also keep well and will be at winter farmers markets until spring. And cooking with dried fruit is another interesting way to vary dessert time.

At the very end of winter, the maple sap will start to flow, and it will be maple syrup season! Time to visit your local sap house, or even to tap your own tree if you have one—it's actually very easy to do. And by then, it will be spring again!

4 large sweet potatoes
½ cup olive oil
Salt and pepper to taste
¼ cup red wine, sherry, or cider vinegar
1 red bell pepper, cored, seeded and quartered
2 teaspoons ground cumin
1 tablespoon grated orange zest
½ cup thinly-sliced scallions
½ cup minced fresh mint, parsley or cilantro leaves
1 or 2 fresh minced chili peppers of your choice, or to taste

Preheat the oven to 400°F. Peel the sweet potatoes and cut them into bite-sized pieces. Put them on a baking sheet, drizzle with 2 tablespoons of the oil and toss to coat. Sprinkle with salt and pepper and roast, turning occasionally, until crisp and brown outside and just tender inside, about 30 minutes. Remove and leave on the pan until ready to dress.

Meanwhile, with a countertop or stick blender, purée the remaining 6 tablespoons oil, vinegar, bell pepper, cumin and zest until smooth. Add salt and pepper to taste.

Toss the warm potatoes with the scallion, green herbs and chiles. Add ½ cup of the dressing and toss to coat, adding more if necessary. Taste and adjust the seasoning. Serve immediately or at room temperature.

4 servings

Peppy Sweet Potato Salad with Red Peppers

A sunny dish that cheats on the season a litte, although you could definitely use frozen local red pepper if you have it.

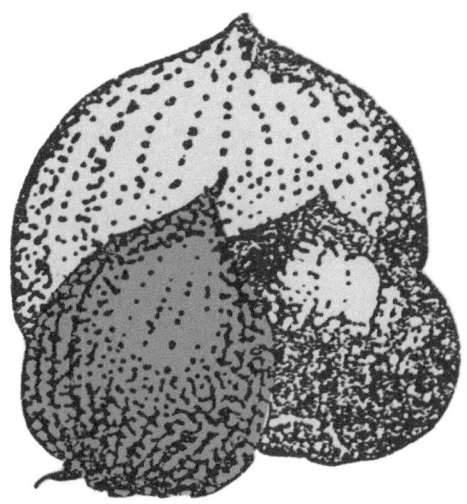

Aroma- therapy Kale, Bean and Farro Soup with Citrus

An exotic stew, perfect for a hearty winter lunch or dinner.

¾ cup dried beans or one 15-ounce can of beans (light-colored will look best)
About 7 cups vegetable, mushroom or light meat stock
¼ cup olive oil
3 oil-packed anchovy fillets, minced
2 teaspoons fresh rosemary, minced
3 garlic cloves, minced or pressed
1 large onion, chopped
1 large carrot, chopped
1 pound kale, dinosaur or other, stems removed and greens roughly chopped*
2 teaspoons salt
¾ cup farro or barley
Pepper
¾ cup coarsely chopped parsley leaves
Grated zest of 1 small lemon
Grated zest of 1 small orange

To cook dried beans: In a medium-small pot, cover beans with water adding 2 more inches. Soak beans overnight or bring to boil for 1 minute and soak for 2 hours.** Replace water with fresh, then simmer on very low heat, covered, until just tender, not soft, timing depends upon the beans chosen.

Drain and reserve up to 1 cup of liquid from cooked or canned beans. Purée half the beans and the reserved cooking liquid in food processor or with blender, adding stock if necessary, to create a thick purée.

Heat the olive oil in a soup pot over medium heat and add all the anchovies, ¾ of the garlic and rosemary, the onion and carrot and stir until soft, about 5 minutes.

Add stock, kale greens, salt, pureed and whole beans, and farro or barley. Bring to a boil.

Reduce heat, cover and simmer until kale and grain are tender, about 25 to 45 minutes. Taste and season as needed.

Combine remaining garlic, rosemary, the orange and lemon zest and parsley. Sprinkle over hot soup or pass at the table.

* To remove stems from kale, either strip it with your hand or fold the leaf in half and cut it with a knife.

** If your water is hard, add a pinch of salt to the soaking water, then a pinch of baking soda before cooking.

6 servings

1 cup loosely packed dried tomatoes (if packed in oil, drain well)
1 28-ounce can whole peeled tomatoes
¼ cup olive oil (or oil from tomatoes)
1 tablespoon minced or pressed garlic
1 medium carrot, finely diced
1 small red onion, halved and finely chopped
Salt and pepper to taste
2 tablespoons honey
1 quart vegetable stock, chicken stock or water
1 tablespoon fresh thyme leaves or 1 teaspoon dried
¼ cup chopped parsley

Put the dried tomatoes in a bowl and cover with 2 cups boiling water (no need if oil packed).

Optional roasting step: Preheat the oven to 375°F. Drain the canned tomatoes, reserving the juice. Halve them and put in a shallow roasting pan; drizzle with 2 tablespoons of the oil. Roast, turning once or twice, until the tomatoes are dried and lightly browned, about 30 minutes. Drain the dried tomatoes and pour their soaking liquid (or some of the juice) into the roasting pan. Use a spoon to scrape all the browned bits from the pan, breaking up the roasted tomatoes.

Put the remaining olive oil in a deep skillet or medium pot over medium-high heat. Add the garlic and cook just until it begins to color, a minute or so. Add the carrot and onion and cook about 3 minutes more.

Sprinkle with salt and pepper, then add the honey and the reserved canned tomato juice and continue stirring until the liquid dries out and begins to brown, about 5 minutes.

Roughly chop the dried tomatoes and add them to the pot. Stir in the stock, the canned tomatoes and the thyme. Turn the heat to high, bring the soup to a boil then lower the heat so it bubbles gently. Cover and cook until the vegetables are very tender, about 30 minutes. Sprinkle with the parsley and serve.

4 servings

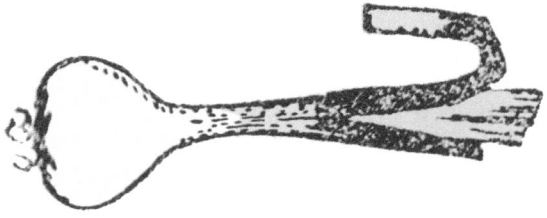

Wintertime Sun Tomato Soup

A robust winter soup with hints of September. Add more vegetables and/or grain for full meal soup. Roasting adds an extra layer of flavor, but if you're pressed for time you can skip it.

The Real Deal Sauerkraut

It amazes me how easy it is to make sauerkraut. And lacto-fermented foods are so good for you, too!

1 large, firm, green or red cabbage, about 5 pounds
3 tablespoons sea salt or 1½ ounces Kosher salt (not iodized)
1 teaspoon caraway seeds (optional)

Remove ragged leaves from the cabbage. Cut it in quarters and remove the core.* Slice the quarters as thinly as possible, making about 5 cups of shredded cabbage. Put into a bowl with the sea salt and work into the cabbage with your fingers until the cabbage begins to release juices. Pack and press it into a non-reactive container, such as a 2-quart glass jar. Add juice; if there's not enough to cover the cabbage, top it up with a brine made from 1 cup filtered water and 1 tablespoon of sea salt.

Place a weight over the cabbage to keep it submerged under the brine.** Cover the jar loosely with a dish towel and let it ferment at room temperature for 1 week or so. Skim any floating bubbles or other matter. Taste the sauerkraut. If you like the flavor, remove the weight, cover the jar and refrigerate. Otherwise, let it continue to ferment until it develops the desired flavor. The sauerkraut will keep in the refrigerator for up to 6 weeks.

Makes about 1 quart

*My mom always gave me the salted core as a special treat.

**The weight can be anything clean and heavy such as a small plate with a scrubbed stone or pie weights; it works to use nesting containers, too. The important thing is to hold the cabbage down below the level of the brine.

Reassuring Braised Cabbage

Another delicious spin on a winter staple that the English call "the prince of vegetables."

2 tablespoons olive oil or butter
1 small cabbage, preferably Savoy, shredded (see sauerkraut, above)
Salt and pepper to taste
½ cup white wine
1 teaspoon maple syrup, honey or brown sugar
¼ teaspoon nutmeg

Put the oil or butter in a large, deep skillet over medium heat. Add the cabbage and stir until it begins to brown, about 5 minutes.

Add salt, pepper and wine, bring back to a simmer, stirring, then add the sugar and nutmeg. Cover and simmer until tender, about 15 minutes. Check the seasoning and serve.

4 servings

2 tablespoons butter or neutral vegetable oil

2 pounds red cabbage (small head), trimmed and shredded (see sauer-kraut, page 54)

3 whole cloves

5 medium apples, peeled or not, cored and cut into chunks

Salt and pepper to taste

½ cup vegetable stock, white wine, apple cider or water (more if needed)

1 tablespoon lemon juice or cider vinegar

Heat the oil in a large skillet or saucepan over medium heat. Add the cabbage and the cloves and cook, stirring until the cabbage becomes soft but not brown, about 20 minutes. Add the apple chunks, sprinkle with salt and pepper, and cook for a couple of minutes while stirring.

Add the stock, turn the heat down and cook, stirring occasionally until the cabbage is tender and the apples are soft, adding more liquid if needed, about 15 minutes. Add the lemon juice or vinegar, taste and adjust the seasoning, and serve.

8 servings

Homey Red Cabbage with Apples

A delicious sweet-and-sour dish, great with corn bread.

Rowdy Roasted Root Vegetables

A great way to warm the kitchen and your guests. The variations make this master recipe infinitely variable.

3 medium carrots, peeled and cut into ½-inch slices
1 small celery root (celeriac), peeled, quartered, cut into ½-inch slices
2 medium parsnips, peeled and cut into ½-inch slices
Salt and pepper to taste
Olive oil

Preheat the oven to about 400°F (flexible!).

Cut the vegetables into pieces that are about the same size so they will cook in the same amount of time.

In a low-sided baking sheet, toss together the vegetables and just enough oil to coat them. Sprinkle with salt and pepper.

Roast, stirring occasionally, until tender, about 25 minutes.

VARIATIONS:
- Use other firm, dry vegetables, such as rutabagas, kohlrabi, cauliflower or turnips.
- Toss the vegetables with leaves of fresh marjoram, thyme, rosemary, savory or crushed cumin or fennel seed along with the salt and oil.
- While still hot from the oven, toss the vegetables with pressed or minced garlic and/or chopped parsley or other herbs.

4 servings

Balsamic Glazed Onions

A great recipe to make when you're out of fresh vegetables. So delicious you'll also make it when you're not.

3 very large yellow onions
4 tablespoons olive oil
3 tablespoons balsamic vinegar
Coarse salt and pepper to taste

Preheat the oven to 400°F.

Peel the onions and cut them in half horizontally. Place cut-side down in heavy shallow casserole. Pour 2 tablespoons of the oil over the onions. Add a sprinkling of coarse salt and pepper.

Bake 20 minutes. The cut side of onions may be black because the sugars have carmelized. Turn over and flatten with a spatula and bake another 15 minutes. Turn again, flatten and bake another 20 minutes until soft and caramelized.

Remove the onions to a serving dish. Add the remaining 2 tablespoons oil and the vinegar to the pan and scrape and stir the browned bits into the mixture. Pour the juices over the onions. Serve warm or at room temperature.

4 servings

56

2 tablespoons nut oil (walnut, hazelnut, etc.) or olive oil
2 medium leeks
4 medium carrots, peeled
6 medium mushrooms, any type, minced
1 teaspoon fresh thyme or ½ teaspoon dried thyme
Salt and pepper to taste

Preheat oven to 400°F.

Tear four 1-foot lengths of aluminum foil. Spread 1 teaspoon oil on half of each. *

Trim the roots and dark green leaf tops from leeks and slice lengthwise in half. Lay cut side down and slice across into 1-inch lengths. Rinse well, checking for dirt and drain. Divide evenly among foil squares.

Cut carrots into 1-inch slices. Distribute among the leeks. Toss the mushrooms with thyme, salt and pepper, then add remaining 2 teaspoons of oil and mix well. Divide evenly among the packets. Fold over foil and form half-moon packets, crimping edges tightly.

Bake in center of oven on a baking sheet for 20 minutes, or until tender. Serve hot.

*Rather than cooking in packets, you could use a tightly covered casserole or baking dish.

4 servings

Oven-Steamed Carrots, Leeks and Mushrooms

Cooking food in packets is fun and transforms mixed veggies into a fragrant mélange.

Maple Glazed Parsnips

Parsnips are the bomb— amazing flavor! This is a sweet-sour dish.

10 medium parsnips, about 2 pounds
1½ tablespoons peanut or vegetable oil
Salt and pepper to taste
½ cup boiling water
2 tablespoons maple syrup
2½ tablespoons balsamic or cider vinegar or a combination
Lemon juice

Preheat oven to 400°F.

Peel parsnips. Cut diagonally into ½-inch slices.

In a roasting pan large enough to hold them in a single layer, toss parsnips with oil and salt to coat. Add water and place in the oven.

Roast until tender, turning every 10 to 15 minutes until easily pierced with a fork. Timing varies from 30 to 60 minutes, depending upon the parsnips. Add a little water if they're drying out.

Drizzle with maple syrup and both vinegars; toss gently. Roast until deeply browned and glazed, turning once or twice, about 10 minutes. Taste and add lemon juice as desired for tartness. Pepper liberally. Serve hot or warm.

4 servings

58

5 medium parsnips, about a pound
1 cup cooked brown rice
Salt and pepper to taste
6 tablespoons (¾ stick) butter, melted
2 tablespoons minced fresh chives for garnish

Parsnip and Brown Rice Rosti

Inspired by Mark Bittman, this yummy take on a Swiss dish is fun to try with different grains. Grating the cooked parsnips is not much fun, but the result is worth it.

Bring a large pot of generously salted water to a boil. Peel and cut the parsnips to fit in the pot. Cook, checking once or twice, until they can be pierced with a tip of a knife but there's still some resistance, just 10 to 15 minutes. Drain and set aside to cool.

Put the brown rice in a large bowl, sprinkle with salt and pepper, and drizzle with 2 tablespoons of the butter. Toss lightly.

Coarsely grate the parsnips, using a food processor if you have one. Place them into a strainer and use a large spoon or a potato masher to press down on them and squeeze out as much water as possible. Add them to the bowl with the rice and toss just enough to combine. Taste and adjust the seasoning.

Put 2 tablespoons of the remaining butter in a deep skillet over medium-high heat. When the butter is beginning to brown, add the rice mixture, firmly pressing it into the pan to form a solid cake. Turn the heat down to low and cook, undisturbed, until the rosti starts to smell toasted, 20 to 25 minutes.

Remove the lid, put a large dish over the skillet, and flip the rosti onto it Add the remaining 2 tablespoons butter to the pan, swirl it around, and turn the heat up to medium and brown it. Slide the rosti into the skillet, raw side down. Leave the skillet uncovered and cook the second side for about 10 minutes or so, checking to make sure it's browned. Slide the finished rosti back onto the plate and sprinkle with chives. Serve hot or at room temperature, cut into wedges.

4 servings

Beet Rosti with Rosemary

Another amazing rosti, this one with a magic combination of beets, rosemary and browned butter.

4 to 5 medium beets, 1 to 1½ pounds
1 teaspoon fresh rosemary, coarsley chopped
1 teaspoon salt
¼ cup flour
2 tablespoons butter

Trim, peel and grate the beets with a hand grater or food processor. Preheat a medium to large non-stick skillet over medium heat.

Toss the beets in a bowl with the rosemary and salt, add the flour slowly, tossing to mix.

Put one tablespoon of butter in a non-stick or well-seasoned skillet and heat and watch until it turns nut-brown. Pour the beet mixture into the skillet, shape it into a nice circle and press it down with a spatula. Turn the heat to medium and cook, covered, shaking the pan occasionally, until the bottom of the beet cake is crisp, 8 to 10 minutes. Put a large plate over the skillet and flip it over. Brown the remaining tablespoon of butter, then slide the cake back into the skillet. Continue to cook, uncovered, lowering the heat if necessary, until the second side is crisp. Cut into wedges and serve hot or room temperature.

4 servings

Roasted Chickpeas

An addicting snack, starter or side dish.

2 cups cooked or canned chickpeas
3 tablespoons olive or neutral oil (grapeseed or corn)
1 tablespoon minced garlic
Salt and pepper to taste

Preheat the oven to 400°F.

Drain and rinse the chickpeas and dry them either in a salad spinner or on a towel.

Put the oil in an ovenproof skillet large enough to hold the chickpeas in one layer and warm over medium heat. When hot, add the chickpeas and garlic and sprinkle with salt and pepper. Shake the pan so that all the chickpeas are well coated with oil and are sitting in one layer.

Transfer the skillet or pan to the oven and roast, shaking the pan occasionally, until the chickpeas begin to brown, 15 or 20 minutes. Remove from the oven and cool slightly.

2 cups

5 medium sweet potatoes
2 tablespoons good quality curry powder or garam masala
Salt to taste
2 tablespoons olive oil

Preheat the oven to 400°F.

Peel the potatoes and cut them into 1-inch chunks. Place them in a medium-size, shallow casserole, sprinkle with the curry powder and salt and drizzle with olive oil.

Bake the potatoes for 45 minutes, turning them once or twice so they brown evenly and don't stick. Serve immediately.

4 servings

4 medium sweet potatoes
1 or 2 celery stalks
1 or 2 small fresh green chiles
¾ teaspoon salt
2 cups water
½ tablespoon curry powder
1 tablespoon minced or grated ginger
1 garlic clove, minced or pressed
1 bunch of kale, about a pound, thick stems removed, chopped
½ cup coconut milk
Lime, lemon or grapefruit wedges

Peel sweet potatoes and cut into ¾-inch dice. Chop the celery. Stem chili, seed, devein (if desired) and mince.

Combine chili, water, salt, curry, ginger and garlic in a pot and bring to a boil. Add potatoes and celery and simmer, covered, for 10 minutes add the kale and cook until potatoes are tender, about 15 minutes. Uncover and simmer to thicken sauce a little. Turn heat to low, add coconut milk and heat for a few minutes to blend flavors.

Serve hot, garnished with citrus wedges.

4 servings

Dry Rubbed Curried Sweet Potatoes

A nice alternative to fried potatoes.

Coconut Curried Sweet Potatoes and Kale

Serve over cooked grain and it's a fast meal.

Marinated White Beans

Fantastic appetizer!

1 cup dried white beans, such as great northern or cannellini
1 quart water
1 bay leaf
2 cloves garlic
½ cup olive oil
½ cup vinegar, tarragon, white wine or sherry are nice here
3 to 4 tablespoons parsley, chopped
½ teaspoon dried oregano, crushed
½ teaspoon dried basil, crushed
¼ teaspoon dried tarragon, crushed
Salt and pepper to taste

Wash the beans, put them in a pot with water to cover plus 2 inches. Either soak them overnight or bring them to a boil and soak for at least one hour.* Drain. Combine the beans with the water, bay leaf, garlic, olive oil and a pinch of salt. Simmer over low heat until they are just tender, 1½ to 2½ hours, testing by tasting. When beans are done, drain them and remove the bay leaf and garlic cloves.

Mix together the rest of the ingredients in a medium bowl and add the beans. They should be just covered. Cover and refrigerate overnight. Serve at room temperature.

* If you have hard water, add a pinch of salt to the soaking water and a pinch of baking soda to the cooking water.

6 servings

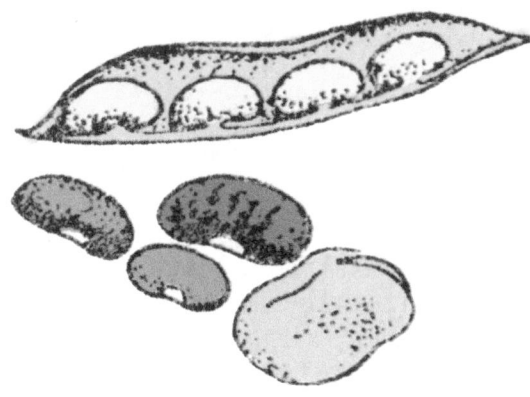

1 pound (3 cups) dried white beans, such as great northern or cannellini or 3 15 oz. cans of white beans
¼ cup butter
1 small onion, chopped
2 cloves garlic, minced or pressed
1 teaspoon fresh thyme or ½ teaspoon dried thyme
2 tablespoons fresh parsley, chopped
1 bay leaf
1½ cups tomato sauce
1 cup dry red wine
Salt and pepper to taste
Big dash of Worcestershire sauce

If cooking dried beans, wash the beans, put them in a pot with water to cover plus 2 inches. Either soak them overnight, or bring them to a boil and soak for at least one hour.* Drain. Pour them into a large pot, add water to cover plus 1 inch.* Simmer gently for 1½ to 2 hours or until the beans are tender. Drain, reserving 1 cup of the liquid.

Meanwhile, preheat the oven to 325°F. In a medium size cooktop- and oven-safe casserole, pot or Dutch oven, melt the butter and sauté the chopped onion until it is tender. Add the garlic, thyme, parsley and bay leaf, the tomato sauce, the liquid from the beans and water to equal 1 cup, and the wine. Simmer for at least 20 minutes or until it is slightly thickened and reduced. Season with salt, lots of pepper and a shake of Worcestershire sauce.

Pour the beans into the sauce, mix well. Cover the pot and bake for 1 to 1½ hours. Serve hot.

* If you have hard water, add a pinch of salt to the soaking water and a pinch of baking soda to the cooking water.

6 servings

Baked Beans a la Charente

This adaptation of Emma Thomas' recipe is a bit involved but so worth it — it's warm, rich and aromatic on a cold winter night.

Pasta with Caramelized Onions

The meal to make when you think you don't have anything to eat.

5 or 6 medium to large onions (about 2 pounds)
⅓ cup olive oil
Salt and pepper to taste
1 pound of long pasta
Grated Parmesan cheese

Thinly slice the onions with a knife, mandolin or food processor. Put a large dry nonstick or well-seasoned skillet over medium-low heat, add the onions and cover. Check and stir every few minutes. The onions will first get wet, then dry out. After they begin to brown and stick to the pan, remove the cover. Add ⅓ cup of olive oil, salt and pepper. Turn the heat up a little.

While the onions continue to cook, bring a large pot of salted water to a boil. Cook the pasta until it is about three-quarters done. Save a cup of pasta water, then drain.

Taste the onions and adjust the seasoning. Add the pasta to the onions, along with a little of the pasta water. Cook until the pasta is tender, adding water as necessary. Mix with some Parmesan and serve, passing more cheese at the table.

4 servings

Frozen Maple Souffle

Fun in February during sugaring season.

1 packet unflavored gelatin granules (1 scant tablespoon)
2 cups maple syrup
2 cups heavy cream, whipped

Dissolve the gelatin in ½ cup cold water. Bring the maple syrup to a boil. Lower the heat and add the gelatin. Cook 2 minutes while stirring. Let stand until mixture begins to thicken. Slowly fold syrup into whipped cream, mixing gently. Pour into glasses or a glass bowl and freeze.

6 servings

3 cups milk (cow, soy, rice or nut)
½ cup maple syrup or sugar
Pinch salt
4 tablespoons (½ stick) unsalted butter, plus more butter for the pan
8 thick slices day-old bread, crusts removed if very thick
3 eggs
2 cups cored, chopped apples, peeled or not
1½ teaspoons ground cardamom

Preheat the oven to 350°F.

Put the milk, sugar, salt and butter in a small saucepan over low heat or in a heatproof cup or bowl in the microwave. Warm just until the butter melts. Meanwhile, butter bottom and sides of a 9-inch round or 8-inch square baking dish that will nest into a larger baking pan (see below). Cut, slice or tear the bread into bite-sized pieces and put in the dish.

Pour the warm milk over. Let it sit for a few minutes, pushing down the floaters. Beat the eggs and stir them into the bread mixture along with the apples and cardamom. Set the baking dish in a larger baking pan and pour enough hot water into the large pan to come up about an inch from the top of the inner dish.

Bake for 45 to 60 minutes or until a knife inserted into the center comes out nearly clean; the center should be just a little soft. Serve hot or at room temperature.

6 to 8 servings

Dutch Baby with Apples

A nice and not- too- complicated brunch dish. Not sure how it got its name, but it's kind of fits.

Pancake:
  3 large eggs
  ¾ cup milk
  ¾ cup white or whole wheat flour
  ½ teaspoon salt
  1½ tablespoon butter
Filling:
  3 medium-sized tart apples, peeled or not
  ¼ cup melted butter
  ¼ cup maple syrup, honey or sugar
  Powdered cinnamon and nutmeg
Topping:
  2 tablespoons melted butter (optional)
  Powdered sugar

Preheat the oven to 450°F.

Beat together the eggs, milk, flour and salt until smooth. In a heavy 12-inch nonstick or well-seasoned oven-safe skillet, melt about 1½ tablespoons butter. When it is hot, pour in the batter and put the skillet in the oven. After 15 minutes, check for large bubbles and pierce with a fork, then lower the oven temperature to 350°F and continue baking for another 10 minutes until light brown and crisp.

While the baby is baking, prepare the filling. Core and thinly slice the apples. In a medium or large skillet, sauté them in ¼ cup butter for a couple of minutes, then add syrup, sugar or honey. Season with cinnamon and nutmeg. The fruit should be just tender.

When the pancake is done, slide it onto a large plate, fill with apples, then flop over to fold in half. Drizzle with melted butter and sprinkle with powdered sugar. Serve hot!

2 to 3 servings

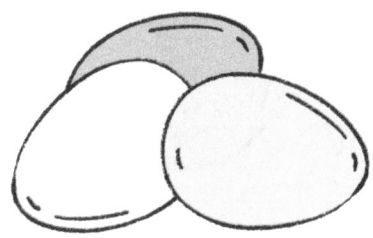

66

2 cups mixed dried fruit
1¾ cups orange or other juice
3 strips of orange zest

Cook over medium heat until the fruit us plump and juicy, 3 to 10 minutes.

4 servings

½ pound (2 sticks) unsalted* butter, softened (more for pan)
1 cup all-purpose flour
1 cup cornmeal
1½ teaspoons baking powder
Pinch salt
1 cup sugar
5 eggs, separated
1 teaspoon vanilla extract

Preheat the oven to 325°F. Butter a 9 x 5-inch loaf pan.

Combine the flour, cornmeal, baking powder and salt in a bowl. In a second bowl, cream the butter. Add ¾ cup of sugar and beat until pale and fluffy, scraping down the sides of the bowl. This takes about 5 minutes—don't cheat. Beat in egg yolks and vanilla.

Mix in the dry ingredients by hand just until smooth and not a second more. In a separate bowl, beat the egg whites until they foam; sprinkle in the remaining ¼ cup sugar while beating to soft peaks. Fold the whites gently but thoroughly into the batter using a large spatula.

Pour into the loaf pan and bake until a toothpick inserted in the center comes out clean, about 1 hour and 15 minutes. After 5 minutes, remove it from the pan and let cool before slicing.

* If you have salted butter, use it, but leave out the pinch of salt.

1 loaf

Cornmeal Pound Cake

So rich with a wonderful texture. Perfect with fruit. This recipe uses three bowls, but it's foolproof.

Index

Uncorrected Proof

CPSIA information can be obtained at www.ICGtesting.com
Printed in the USA
BVOW10s0449090415

395388BV00004B/4/P